AMERICA'S
HOUSING
CHALLENGE

Also by Roger Starr

Roger Starr

AMERICA'S
HOUSING
CHALLENGE

What It Is and How to Meet It

A NEW LEADER BOOK

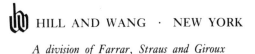 HILL AND WANG · NEW YORK

A division of Farrar, Straus and Giroux

This book is a revised and expanded version of a special issue of *The New Leader*. Conceived by the editors of the magazine, it was produced under a grant from the Tamiment Institute. It is the second in a series sponsored by the foundation that will deal with a variety of subjects related to matters of social welfare.

First printing, 1977

Published simultaneously in Canada by
McGraw-Hill Ryerson Ltd., Toronto
Printed in the United States of America
Designed by Nanette Stevenson

Library of Congress Cataloging in Publication Data

Starr, Roger.
    America's housing challenge.

    "A New Leader book."
    "A revised and expanded version of a special issue of The New Leader."
    Includes index.
    1. Housing—United States. I. The New Leader.
II. Title.
HD7293.S659   1977   301.5'4'0973   77-7108

CONTENTS

AMERICA'S
HOUSING
CHALLENGE

INTRODUCTION

Although no one seems prepared to say so, the American housing achievement since World War II has been mighty, ending the days when a President of the United States could describe a third of the nation as ill-housed. The tremendous net increase in the number of standard dwellings reflects the enormous amount of resources—land, materials, labor, and capital—devoted to housing over the past three decades.

A significant part of the success has been due to public policy. The federal government accepted responsibility for a national housing program in 1937, a decision practically obliterated by the outbreak of World War II; but the commitment was renewed in 1949, when the act sponsored by Senators Wagner, Ellender, and Taft set a national goal of 810,000 publicly owned, subsidized housing units and launched the major effort now known as urban renewal.

The postwar years have seen, as well, vast private accomplishments in housing, sometimes with government help in the form of mortgage insurance but more often not. These have changed the very look of the United States. Immense suburbs have risen where no one lived before; new apartment complexes have appeared across the land; most of the rural shacks that disgraced the right-of-way of every major Southern highway have disappeared. As a result of direct public involvement, the character of some of the most depressing urban slums has been drastically altered, and major emphasis has been placed on racial integration.

Institutional changes have occurred, too. State and local governments have established agencies for financing housing developments. A federal Department of Housing and Urban Development has emerged. Mortgage institutions, most notably the Savings and Loan Associations—with their affiliated Federal Home Loan Bank Board—have grown to a size no one had expected. Other national agencies have been set up to assist the marketing of mortages and to encourage capital investment in housing.

The effects of all this activity are evident in the 1970 Census figures. While no one is quite clear about what precisely defines a substandard unit, the simplest test remains dilapidation or absence of full plumbing. By these criteria the third of the nation found to be ill-housed in 1936 had dropped to less than one tenth in 1970. Substandard units dropped by 8 million and the total number of dwelling units increased by 10 million during the 1960s alone. The Census further reported that only 15 percent of the country's dwelling units were overcrowded, using the very rigorous standard of one person per room.

In spite of these statistics, the public perception of American housing indicates continuing dissatisfaction, both with the shape and quality of new, largely private tract housing developments and with the work already accomplished or remaining still undone in the older cities. And for good reason. Leaving aside the perhaps overintellectualized condemnation of the new one-family homes, no visitor wandering through the mean streets of the South Bronx, or viewing the Dorchester section of Boston, or poking his way about parts of Woodlawn in Chicago, or touring sections of Philadelphia, Washington, San Antonio, Oakland, or a dozen other U.S. cities, large and small, would take very much pride in the nation's housing achievement. Obviously, the Census figures must be adjusted to produce a complete picture of the remaining problem.

To begin with, the Bureau of the Census tallies the presence of plumbing fixtures, but it does not report whether they are actually working or whether they will be six months hence (a significant question for inflationary times because the deterioration of existing housing quickens with the pace of rising costs). Then, too, census takers do not count abandoned buildings (no one lives in them to answer questions) or estimate the rate at which usable buildings may become abandoned, as sometimes happens without clear warning. For example, there is now an empty lot in the Hunt's Point section of the Bronx at the very address where the city not long ago invested $400,000 in a loan to rehabilitate a tenement house; within three years of its rehabilitation the building was demolished as a physical danger to the neighborhood.

Similarly, the Census fails to record the qualities of the decaying buildings in the side streets, or the miserable quasi-hotels where hundreds of thousands of elderly Americans subsist on their Social Security and SSI payments. Nor does it remind us that the 10 percent of the population which is living in patently substandard housing amounts to approximately 20 million people. Nor does it note, in an easily assimilable form, that this national average becomes a much larger proportion of the population if one subtracts from the total the unblighted new suburbs and the booming urban growth areas and focuses instead on the multiple dwellings that are over seventy-five years old or are located in neighborhoods where racial shifts have changed investment patterns. Nor do the statistics tell us how many families are about to live in unsatisfactory housing because their incomes cannot keep pace with the rents needed to cover the cost of operating the buildings they occupy at present.

The contrast between New York City tenement houses and luxury apartments was dramatized by Sidney Kingsley in *Dead End* in 1934. In 1977, disparity between the quality of housing in the new suburbs and in inner-city ghettos remains, but the adjacent polar opposites of very rich and very poor that provided the dramatic confrontation of *Dead End* have become more subtle. The new tract housing suburbs are not a province of the wealthy, but of middle-class union members, small businessmen, subprofessionals, and junior (in rank, not age) private and governmental employees.

Steady improvement in the quality of housing enjoyed by this immensely wide band of Americans has made it more rather than less difficult to summon the resources and political will power to alleviate the deprivation of those forced to live in substandard older urban dwellings. Whereas reformist efforts in housing were formerly intended to benefit the working population at the purported expense of the rich, further progress will necessarily benefit the nonworking poor at an apparent cost to the power, the comfort, and even the safety of the working class.

The high correlation that remains in 1977 between bad housing and low income and membership in a minority group carries an unmistakable political message: The poor can no longer expect to obtain better homes in the wake of a general drive to improve housing standards for the middle class, as was the case during the first twenty years after World War II. The poor are not nearly as well represented as the more numerous, politically more active working class.

A recent study by the Harvard-MIT Joint Center on Urban Affairs emphasizes yet another aspect of housing inequality: the portion of income that must be spent on housing by Americans of different income. At the very top of the economic pyramid, the wealthiest and most extravagantly housed families allocate less than 10 percent, often less than 5 percent, of their budgets to housing. The percentage is low because there are limits to the amount any family can spend on housing. Secondly, home-owning families (including those who occupy cooperative or condominium apartments) may deduct their mortgage interest and real property taxes from their gross income before calculating their taxes, thus further reducing the percentage of their income devoted to housing. Some economists would apply an even sterner test to the cost inequalities of housing. Henry Aaron of the Brookings Institution believes that home-owning families are being given a mammoth subsidy because the government fails to tax them on the income they might be deemed to receive if they paid themselves rent for the use of their own houses. This "imputed rent," according to Aaron, means that the federal treasury forgoes a possible $10 billion in income taxes annually, and increases the disparity in the cost of housing between the wealthy and the poor. The imputed rent theory is controversial among economists, and it can be argued that from a practical point of view the societal advantages of home ownership justify this "tax break." Still, there is no denying that the income tax deductibility of directly paid real property taxes and mortgage interest tends to offset the progressive impact of the income tax rates, and this in itself constitutes an inequity.

Thus, despite the magnificent accomplishments in housing of the past thirty years, major problems remain; they center on the way our resources have been distributed. This raises the very real question of whether it is possible to improve the distribution pattern and thereby reduce the existing inequality. The answer is that we must face the first reality of housing: It is extremely expensive.

For purposes of illustration, let us assume that the total development cost of an apartment in a fireproof building on New York's Lower East Side, lived in by a family of four whose wage earner is an unskilled hospital worker earning $8,500 annually, is $45,000. The basic expense of running the five-room apartment, without considering interest on the original investment or taxes, comes to $310 per room per year. If the $8,500 worker were to pay for the total cost of his apartment, it would consume more than 60 percent of his gross income.

In an industrialized society, housing is by far the most

complex item the economy is asked to supply for the exclusive use of a single individual or family. In the temperate zone occupied by the United States, adequate shelter involves more than a roof over one's head. It must shield its occupants against heat and cold, against snow, rain, and wind, against fire and burglary. Moreover, local, state, and national governments have entered the marketplace by enacting very specific building and housing codes that impose minimum standards on the builder, both to protect the buyer from shoddy construction and to protect the community against fire, plague, and other hazards.

In an industrialized society, housing may be regarded as a bundle of three packages. In addition to the shelter package, housing must include a utility package, comprising all the external services modern life depends upon: electricity, running water and a network of pipes and reservoirs, and the transportation system that moves people to their work, their schools, their recreation. It encompasses also such public services as the police, fire, health, and sanitation departments.

Lastly there is the social package. If housing is to be of use to anyone except perhaps an eccentric descendant of Henry David Thoreau, it cannot stand in isolation, but must offer its occupants a setting in which to live their lives. The social package begins with access to a way of earning a livelihood and extends to the environment that reflects the values of the immediate social group in a particular residential area. Educational institutions form a very important part of the living environment; next after jobs, Americans tend to choose housing on the basis of the educational opportunities its location will make available to their children. Generally speaking, when people say they want to live in a "good" neighborhood, they mean that they want to live among those who resemble them in income, education, and cultural aspirations.

The utility and social packages bear most importantly on the formulation of national policy. As we shall see, the cost of the utility package is a vital consideration in deciding whether the federal government should favor the rehabilitation of existing older cities or the creation of new utility packages on vacant or near-vacant lands outside. This, in turn, involves matters of social policy, including the place of socioeconomic distinctions in American life and the connection between racial discrimination and social class. One of the major frustrations in the actual execution of public housing policy arises from the fact that few officials dare admit in public that no answers to these questions now exist.

For obvious political reasons, it is difficult to acknowledge openly that no one knows how to create a neighborhood where different social classes will live together harmoniously, unless the area possesses remarkable advantages for which families with a choice would be ready to abandon some of their other natural preferences. Nobody who has responsibility for local housing policy can comfortably state in public that we do not yet have a cure for the emotional problems and behavior patterns of many troubled urban families. No one may base policy on the frank admission that the minority has become the majority in vast sections of our cities and no way has been found to desegregate the schools under such conditions.

In the preamble to the National Housing Act of 1949 (amended frequently), Congress declared that every American family should have not only a "decent" home but a "suitable living environment." The crucial word, "suitable," was probably selected in the hope that it would be neutral in defining the qualities of neighborhoods. With luck, in America people may eventually be willing to accept neighbors who differ from them in color, national origin, and religion. In 1977, however, ethnic and racial considerations help to shape the demand for a specific social package, as do the institutions—schools, churches, movie theaters, clubs, etc.—that give families the opportunity to interact.

The promise of environmental suitability in the preamble to the Housing Act also contains an irony that the nation has so far been unwilling to face: What is to be done with those households or individuals who tend to destroy for others the suitability of the neighborhood to which they have moved?

Another bitter truth about housing, one which emphasizes its inequalities, is that there is little consistency in the way the utility and social packages are financed. Our accounting system for municipal expenditures tends to externalize many utility and social costs of one-family-home neighborhoods. They are covered by government with funds from the general tax rolls. The same costs are internalized in the case of multiple-dwelling elevator structures, so that they must be paid for directly by the residents themselves.

In a private home area, the public street is laid down at the general expense of all local taxpayers, industrial and commercial as well as residential. In an apartment building containing as many individual units as would be found on four or five or more blocks of one-family houses, the elevator transportation that substitutes for the public street is paid for solely by the tenants. In fact, each pays a share of the property tax on the assessed value of the elevator, too, while no one pays a tax on the value of the public street he uses.

As for solid-waste removal, the individual home owner is frequently entitled to public garbage collection, especially if he lives in a large city. The garbage trucks must stop at every house, where the cans or bags of uncompacted and unincinerated waste are hoisted on board. Payment for this service comes from general tax revenues. The apartment house resident must pay rent which includes money to pay for the internal collection of garbage, and often for its incineration or compaction. No one has tried to justify this allocation of the price of the utility package, but a number of writers on urban economics, including Coleman Woodbury, have pointed out that no single-family-home neighborhood contributes enough revenue to the municipal government to cover all the services its residents receive.

The process by which public and private resources are transformed into the housing packages tends to conceal the real costs of different income levels. Any attempt by government to equalize the "hidden" subsidization of housing among all citizens would undoubtedly encounter loud political objections. Private home owners do not like to be informed that apartment house dwellers are taxed more per room than they are, and refuse to understand that the street they get free is the equivalent of an elevator paid for by the tenants of a high rise. Americans, consequently, have been inclined to overemphasize the cost of multistory housing in the central city and to underestimate the total social cost of building on the vacant land outside.

Yet no people can live only on economics. While the questions of where and for whom housing should be built rank among the central public policy concerns of this era, they cannot be separated from what is perhaps the most crucial question of all: What are the proper and practical limits of government action in the social sphere?

With respect to housing, what form of ownership should government favor when it begins to marshal resources for construction, rehabilitation, and maintenance? Resident home ownership? Rental ownership for profit? Public ownership? Mutual ownership as found in cooperatives or condominiums? Eleemosynary ownership? The nature of ownership dictates attention to its corollary, tenure—the occupant's rights in and obligations for the home he inhabits. An evaluation of the condition of our housing must begin with these two fundamental issues, often pontificated about but seldom seriously examined.

I

OWNERSHIP
AND TENURE

Fanciful thinkers may well imagine a world in which home ownership would be unknown, a state of affairs that would satisfy those who characterize property as theft. Human dwellings could be produced like birdhouses, left to be lived in and, one hopes, maintained, by any family of passersby casually searching for a place to settle. One must wonder, however, how long this accidental housing would remain in satisfactory condition if no person or agency were responsible for its upkeep or entitled to expect some long-term benefit from such care. Presumably, anyone would be free to move to another birdhouse whenever he wearied of the one he already occupied.

Ownership, in one form or another, has stood the test of time because it identifies either a real or a merely legal entity as entitled to derive benefit from the long-term care of what belongs to him or it. Thus ownership provides a means of balancing the two contradictory impulses that drive men in relationship to property. The first impulse is to enjoy it to the full for its power to gratify instant desire. The second, more cautionary impulse is to guard it unscathed for future use when its availability may be even more gratifying. The record of how poorly the world balances the consumptive urge against the conservative wisdom in the case of, say, whales—which are no man's property since they inhabit the ownerless sea—suggests that ownership remains an important social tool.

In the case of housing, the conservative urge generally bespeaks the importance of *ownership*; the impulse to enjoy now, immediately, bespeaks the significance of *tenure*. Custom, law, and the social institutions define the rights and obligations conveyed by ownership and by tenure. It is clear that, vested absolutely in different parties, ownership and tenure offer directly opposed motivations. The differences between landlord and tenant are therefore not merely trivial, personal, or transitory; each side seeks very different rewards from the existence of property. The owner gives primary weight to his long-term interest, which in the best of social worlds recommends to him the sound maintenance of his property so that it will produce income without loss of its ultimate sale value. At times of real, threatened, or imagined social change, the conservative impulse tends to curdle. The owner, abandoning belief in a future sale value, tries to turn his property into as much cash income as he can, hoping to pocket as much cash as possible, depending on this, rather than the endangered property, for his long-term security. There may, indeed, be neither present reward nor future benefit in the ownership of residential property for the use of others; the obvious result is the abandonment of property by its owner, a process now continuing (openly) in many older American cities.

The tenant, for his part, concerns himself with the present usefulness of property to him. Obviously he does not care whether the rent he pays is sufficient to maintain the value of the property for the ultimate benefit of its owner. He wants the property well maintained, not for his successor, but rather during the period of his own tenure; he wants his rent to remain fixed because he has long since discovered that the payment of rent for premises already lived in provides little psychological satisfaction. It is much more pleasant to spend on the acquisition of things not previously enjoyed, or on consumption which he hopes will provide him with novel pleasures and previously unattained satisfaction of needs. The tenant wants the strongest possible protection of his tenure; besides wanting his rent to be fixed, he wants his own possession of the premises secure against any interruptions except those of his own making. The owner's view is, equally understandably, directly opposed: he would like to be able to raise rents as costs rise and as the market permits him to (the "sitting" tenant is at a natural disadvantage in the housing market: it costs him money to move as a consequence of resisting the owner's demands for higher rent). Naturally the owner would prefer his tenant's tenure to be as weak as possible. While he is happy to require that the tenant remain and pay his rent during periods of market softness, he would like to be able to recapture possession of the leased premises in order to consummate a sale or get a higher rental.

The opposition of these interests—the owner's and the tenant's—produced in the Western world a long acrimonious history of political opposition and agitation. Indeed, the strife was even more deadly in those centuries when access to agricultural land remained the sole means of economic survival while the rising economic importance of grazing threatened the tenure of the peasant plowman, at least in England. The discovery of America held out to frightened European tenant farmers the promise of sufficient acreage to distribute to each family. Adequate public land resources would permit the opposed forces of landless peasant and landed autocrat to merge into a new entity, the farmer-owner. To use the English term, all agricultural workers would become yeomen. Against this brutal background of land enclosure and peasant rebellion, Americans cherished the hope that each family (whatever its means of earning a living) would own its own home.

In the general affluence, owners and tenants would disappear as separate interests.

Black people were excluded from these expectations, however. They had been brought to America to become part of a wholly different agricultural system: the plantation. Home ownership also lay beyond the reach of a large part of the white population of the growing seaboard cities. For them, working not on land but in the nascent urban factories, the new institution of rental housing gradually developed. The first deliberately planned rental units—"tenant houses," later shortened to "tenements"—did not appear in New York City until the 1840s. In any case, New York City remains the only city in the United States in which most people live as tenants in rented premises containing three families or more. Even so, one- and two-family houses contain nearly 30 percent of the New York City population.

Those who expected that the rolling of the owner and the occupant together into a single interest would provide secure tenure as well as economically sound ownership found reality less simple than this expectation. Even as heating systems and indoor plumbing made tenant housing complex and more expensive to build and maintain, so also economic depressions proved that a large part of the single-family owner-resident stock was vulnerable to a drop in personal income. In 1930, it became all too clear that the owner who had borrowed the money for his home enjoyed only a limited tenure; his continuing power to live in it depended upon his ability to meet the mortgage terms of whatever institution or person had provided the money with which the home had been built.

The Great Depression proved that the institutional mortgage system of the country could not comfortably survive a major drop in average personal income. Depositors in the banks that had made mortgage loans needed to remove their savings because their own income had dropped. Fear that the banks were insufficiently liquid to meet withdrawal orders quickened the pace of attempted withdrawals.

Mortgages had been of the "standing type," meaning that the owner did not reduce the outstanding balance in periodic monthly or quarterly payments. When the lending institutions needed cash to meet withdrawals by their depositors, they refused to renew expiring mortgages, hoping that the owners could pay their debts. When the owners were unable to do so, the bankers moved to foreclose their mortgages, hoping that someone would bid for their properties at ensuing sheriff's sales. Suffering followed on all sides; owner-residents lost their homes, just as tenants with weak tenure were likely to have lost theirs at the whim of owners.

Government simply could not permit this to continue. Essentially, if the United States economy was sound, most of the mortgages that were being foreclosed must be sound too. Unless they had been based on a serious miscalculation of the underlying value or demand for the houses that secured them, the mortgages could be carried by the home owner. If he was working, his income would be ample to pay the debt. Both the Republicans, who were in power when the stock market collapsed in 1929, and the Democrats, who replaced them in 1933, recognized the need for national action. Yet they differed in approach. The Republicans tried to strengthen the credit institutions through the establishment of the Reconstruction Finance Corporation, probably hoping that this would slow down the pace of foreclosure by reducing depositors' panicky demands for cash. The Democrats established the Home Owners' Loan Corporation, which stabilized the situation directly. The HOLC acquired title to a significant number of the houses that were in the process of foreclosure. The HOLC held them, allowing their former owners to remain as tenants. The tenants were given an opportunity to repurchase their homes under revised mortgage terms. Finally, the HOLC sold these new mortgages to financial institutions, emerging years later with a profit which it turned over to the United States Treasury.

The key to this profit could be found in the nature of the mortgage devised by the government. It was a long-term mortgage, far longer than anything that private lenders had been willing to offer, and it provided for monthly amortization of the principal. Monthly payments were set so that, at the end of the mortgage term, the debt would be totally extinguished. The mortgage covered 90 percent or more of the total original cost of the home. This self-amortizing mortgage provided the basis for the postwar housing boom in single-family owner-occupied houses. It was a form of home lending made attractive to financing institutions by government insurance of the mortgage payments, the premiums of which were paid by the borrower. Since the Federal Housing Administration, which wrote the insurance on the mortgages and established the housing standards that governed their insurability, was able to earn a profit on the insurance, many lending institutions began after a while to recognize that the low-down-payment, long-term, fully self-amortizing mortgage was a sound investment. As a result, the great majority of home mortgages in the postwar years were made without FHA insurance, but generally on terms which the FHA had shown to be sound. Defaults ran at a very low figure.

Nevertheless, looking at the surge of new home construction between 1945 and 1976, one must wonder what had happened to make all previous mortgage doctrines look merely cautious. Serious mortgage lenders had previously demanded substantial investment of their own money by owners. With so large a stake of his own in his house, the owner, lenders argued, would be reluctant to risk losing it by failing to make prompt payments. Mortgages traditionally had been made for short terms, such as five or ten years. This period was customarily extended each time a mortgage matured, offering the lender a significant means of protection against increases in the interest rate.

Two unprecedented factors explained the success of the unconventional postwar mortgage. First in importance was the continuous prosperity of the national economy. Unbroken employment at rising wages for the heads of families who had been in the home-owning age bracket immediately after

World War II meant that their income remained indeed sufficient to pay the fixed mortgage costs despite the inflationary rise in building costs and taxes. Furthermore, the owner's equity value in his home increased rapidly; his maximum mortgage debt had been fixed at the outset. Each monthly payment reduced his debt. Meanwhile, the sale value of his house increased almost constantly, as the rise in the number of new families strengthened demand while new houses became constantly more costly to build. The safety of the mortgage lender's money improved as long as these conditions lasted.

The second factor in the success of postwar one-family home construction was the persistence for six years after World War II of an agreement between the Treasury and the Federal Reserve Board to keep general interest rates low so that the national debt would be easier for taxpayers to bear. The lenders who had been fearful that they would be stuck with long-term mortgages at interest rates lower than the dividends they would have to pay their depositors found that they had no better place than home mortgages to put their money.

In periods in which these factors—high employment and stable interest rates—do not coexist, the continuous building of one-family homes on a large scale requires government intervention, to keep mortgage interest rates artificially low. Long-term mortgages cease to attract lenders when they find interest rates rising and hear their depositors' demands for higher returns on their deposits. In recent years, depositors have not bothered to argue with their friendly bankers when they feel that interest rates on their savings are too low; they simply take out their deposits and invest the money in Treasury Bills, or other obligations which are earning higher yields than the savings institutions. Special interest-rate subsidies for mortgages are very expensive to the government and inspire resistance by the Federal Reserve Board when the housing activity threatens to unstabilize wage rates and capital allocations.

The political and economic difficulties in one-family

home construction in all phases of the business cycle are made more complicated by major sociological considerations. In 1942, the late Charles Abrams, writing in his *The Future of Housing*, decried the ideal of universal home ownership as unsound, both economically and sociologically. Home ownership requires the family to put its savings into the ownership of a home. If the nation enters a period in which housing prices stop rising, the ensuing loss of family and bank liquidity could become as serious as in the 1930s. Furthermore, Abrams pointed out, forced saving in a house anchors a family in a place which may not be in the long run appropriate either for the family or for the economy as a whole. Industrialization has required a highly mobile labor force, which American living habits have heretofore provided. And with greater longevity and earlier retirement, many people have more post-employment years at their disposal. As older citizens seek to move southward, they often face difficulty in divesting themselves of their old homes in which they have build up a large equity. Thus, home ownership may thwart what people sense as the achievement of their needs in the period of retirement.

Nevertheless, home ownership does present the advantages that flow from the identity between occupant and owner. Home owners are willing to perform routine maintenance chores themselves, which the tenants of rented accommodations rarely undertake. The owner-occupant does not care whether he performs these chores for his immediate pleasure, so that he can live more comfortably, or whether he performs them to increase the future value of his house; he simply does them. In the process, housing costs which would be charged in dollars to the tenant in rental housing simply disappear from accounting altogether.

Reacting to the rapidly escalating dollar costs of private rental housing, and by his disappointment over some of the other forms of ownership and tenure, the same Charles Abrams who denounced home ownership in 1942 came, by 1964, to assert in *The City Is the Frontier* that universal home ownership was essential to the solution of the housing problems even of the poorest American families.

Whether right or wrong, Abrams' second prescription was nearly as visionary as his first had been. Large sections of the nation's older cities had been developed with multiple-family dwellings, and most of them were owned by people who expected to make money on their operations. Characteristically, the ownership of rental housing had been a business for small-scale entrepreneurs for almost a century after its beginnings in the 1840s. Many based their retirement plans on the properties in which they had invested their money.

As the general level of wealth rose in the nineteenth century, reformists in the larger cities persuaded legislators to impose housing quality standards by law. Beginning with very simple requirements, the housing codes gradually became complex; compliance became more expensive. Gradually, as the capital required to construct housing increased, entrepreneurs had to become more sophisticated in their ability to raise money, operate buildings, and deal with tenants. Clumsier and cruder entrepreneurs lost out. The tenants' tenure in the earliest and simplest rental buildings had been based on handshake month-to-month leases, but in newer buildings, intended for richer occupants, institutional mortgagees—such as savings banks—demanded written contract leases that covered a period of years. Although the ownership industry was fractionalized, and highly competitive in seeking tenants, most owners in the larger cities adopted a standard form of lease, usually one prepared by the local real estate board. The lease was consequently very favorable to the owners, and skimpy in its concessions to tenants. The tenant movement, localized but increasingly powerful, succeeded in the 1960s and 1970s in modifying by statute some of the conditions of the standard lease—the waiver of jury trials has been outlawed, for example.

Rent control drastically changes the tenure of tenants. In most instances, it substitutes a statutory tenure for a contract tenure. Statutory tenure means that the resident in a rental apartment house continues to occupy his home so long as the rent control ordinance permits it. The replacement of contract tenure with a tenure determined by legislation has had the effect of increasing the political activity of tenant groups and has encouraged the rise of tenant leaders in politics. Since tenants inevitably greatly outnumber apartment house owners, legislative enactments tend to favor the interests of tenants, especially in those jurisdictions where rental accommodations constitute a major part of the housing stock. On the other hand, in a tight rental market, with few vacancies, the tenant in residence (in English parlance, the "sitting" tenant) is peculiarly vulnerable to the demands of the owner of his premises as his contract tenure nears its end. It is easier to make demands on the tenant already in residence than to make them on the tenant who is looking for space; the sitting tenant faces peculiar costs if he rejects the proffered new lease. He must bear the expense of moving and relocation.

One curious effect of this weakness of the lessee's tenure has generally been to separate the tenant movement from the housing movement. The tenant movement has concentrated its efforts on rent control, the forms of lease, the enforcement of the housing codes, the procedures of eviction. Meanwhile a consortium of builders, architects, lawyers, social workers, and other interested citizens who may not themselves be tenants at all, have been responsible for generating housing programs, rather than tenant programs. These seek to stimulate construction or rehabilitation of housing and to make this housing available to prospective residents who cannot afford to occupy it without some special economic assistance. In general, the nontenant housing reformists started by exploring forms of ownership and tenure which seemed suitable for the solution of the economic problem of housing; that problem, of course, being the fact that housing adhering to the standards of quality set by the laws sponsored by the reformists was too costly for low-income, working-class families to live in. A general rise in wages rarely helped the wage earner to meet housing costs; the housing costs usually rose faster than wages.

Early analysis of this problem suggested a simple solution; namely, that housing for working-class families should be developed and owned by private philanthropists who would be content to receive only a modest profit from their endeavors. The clear premise of this proposal was that excessive profits demanded by the owners of rental housing were responsible for the high costs. The movement for semicharitable ownership of rental housing—"6 percent philanthropy," as it was called—peaked in the early years of this century. It did produce a number of so-called model apartments in a number of American cities, but soon even the most enthusiastic supporters had to acknowledge that there were too few housing philanthropists to take the measure of the urban housing need. The acceptance of this disappointment was made somewhat easier by two factors that suggested that philanthropic motivation was insufficient to cover the increasing cost of standard housing. First, electricity and a demand for central heating made the new housing far more expensive than it had been without light, heat, or hot water; second, the limited profits failed to provide a cushion against contingent costs, so that the 6 percent first became zero percent. Then it became a loss.

Historically, the philanthropic housing movement, based on ownership by wealthy men with modest tastes, was followed in America by the hope that cooperative ownership would solve the conflict between owner and tenant just as single-family ownership succeeds in doing. Cooperative ownership of multifamily dwellings produced some successes in the 1920s—particularly when the cooperators shared religious affiliation or ties to common institutions like labor unions. While some jointly owned condominiums for well-to-do people flourish, the recent fruits of the national cooperative movement in housing have been disappointingly skimpy.

The major reason for this disappointment is painfully obvious: the wide expansion of the cooperative movement in housing, which started only in very recent years, has not resulted from the educational and promotional activities of the League for Co-operatives or any other organization dedi-

cated to the social benefits of the cooperative mode of ownership. Rather, cooperative housing has been stimulated by
professional builders. In the 1960s, these investors found that
the ownership of rental housing was not very attractive except in the case of housing catering to the very rich or to relatively docile tenants, such as the elderly, or to those, such
as "swinging singles," who were too busy to make their relations with their landlords a central fact of life. Thus, cooperatives and condominiums began to flourish in the 1960s because they offered a way in which the builder could profit
from his judgment in selecting a site, choosing an architect,
and building with relative economy, without having to maintain a permanent investment and deal with family tenancies at
a time of growing consumerist power in the economy generally and in the tenant field particularly.

The financing pattern laid down by the federal government for cooperatives included mortgages covering as much
as 97 percent of costs in the case of certain types and 90 percent in others. State housing finance agencies entered the picture to provide mortgages for cooperatives that covered as
much as 95 percent of development costs. Stimulated by this
credit expansion, significant numbers of these cooperatives
were begun by the late 1960s. They were filled with people
who had no special background in the ethos of the cooperative movement or preparation for the difficulties of assuming
the ownership interest in the long-term soundness of the
apartment house and, at the same time, the tenant's interest
in low rents. Because equity payments were minimal—
amounting in some cases only to a few hundred dollars per
room—many of these new style cooperators continue to feel
that they have simply paid key money for their apartments,
and that they are, in effect, tenants of the government which
insured or made their mortgage rather than tenant-owners
who had simply borrowed from government. As inflation
pushes housing costs upward, many of the new cooperators
are abandoning their ownership interest entirely, and with-
hold rent from their own corporation. Co-op City in New

York, with 15,500 cooperator families, is the outstanding and most notorious instance of this.

It is clear in the brilliant light of hindsight that the cooperative mode of ownership is peculiarly vulnerable to inflationary pressures, just as, during the Great Depression, many "luxury" coops of the rich had proved vulnerable to the pressures of deflation. Cooperation, in short, requires a relatively stable employment and price structure in the economy as a whole, because of the widespread dispersal of the ownership among all of the tenant-cooperators, some of whom are certain to be adversely affected by economic changes. Cooperative corporations whose members have limited personal resources find it extremely difficult to accumulate general reserves. The money collected to establish such reserves simply seems like more rent to the tenant-owners who must pay it. Accordingly, when economic difficulties arise, the lack of a *single* owner with some resources in addition to the apartment house itself accentuates the financial instability of the enterprise.

It is remarkable that several of the union-sponsored cooperative enterprises established in the 1920s in New York City actually did survive the Great Depression and the serious diminution of their members' earnings. That survival depended largely on the leadership of the renowned Abraham Kazan, who came into the housing cooperative movement in the 1920s through his affiliation with the Amalgamated Clothing Workers. Union affiliation and union ideology provided a field in which Kazan's militant leadership could flourish. That his successors in the United Housing Foundation have been unable to continue the leadership and discipline that he inspired is far less a comment on them than on the change in the ideology which the tenant-cooperators bring into the housing that is built for them.

But even in the 1920s, before current disasters manifested themselves, it had become clear that the cooperative housing movement, like a philanthropic profit-making ownership, could not by itself fill the demand for moderate-cost housing for working-class families and others of low income. The profit of the housing owner was not, it turned out, the crucial factor in housing cost; profit was far less important than the cost of the components of a housing unit that was built and maintained in accordance with the legal standards that had gradually been developed. Other important elements in housing costs are the rate of interest charged on the mortgage money that pays for most of the original land and construction cost of the housing, and the continuing local real estate taxes that represent in large part the cost of municipal services and facilities without which housing would be useless.

In short, as long ago as the 1930s, it was becoming obvious that no matter what the form of ownership might be, the kind of housing that legislators demanded for the cities would require subsidization to bring it within the economic reach of the ordinary working-class family. The public policy question which arose from the perception of the need for subsidies was this: to what form of ownership could subsidies safely be paid, so that the effect of their payment would be the reduction of rents rather than the establishment of higher profits at the expense of the taxpayers?

In the 1930s, this public policy issue resulted in the establishment of government-owned housing. While there may have been a lingering belief on the part of some that government ownership was *per se* cheaper than private ownership, the mainspring in the development of publicly owned housing as a national institution was the sense that government ownership alone could guarantee that the major public investment in making housing available for low-income families would not be perverted to greed.

The public housing program that emerged in the 1937 National Housing Act provided, in effect, that the federal government would pay for the entire cost of constructing public housing units, but that these developments would belong to local governments. To qualify for federal help, local governments were required to agree in advance that they would provide all municipal services to the residents of the federally-paid-for projects, even though the projects would be exempted from all local real estate taxes. Subsequently, the federal government permitted the projects to make payments "in lieu of" taxes, usually amounting to approximately 20 percent of what normal *ad valorem* taxes on the new buildings would have been. The tenants were required to pay for all the operating costs of the projects, whether, as in most cases, from their wages or, as in some, from welfare or Social Security payments received by them. The local governments were permitted to establish their own rules about income limitations; most provided that when incomes rose to a stipulated percentage above the maximum income standard for admission, the family would move out, making way for another low-income family. In the meantime, as income rose toward the ceiling, tenants would pay proportionately higher rents.

The public housing program has been bathed in controversy from its beginnings, creating a public opinion atmosphere in which it was quite easy for the Ford administration finally to accept the ban against further construction that was contained in the Housing and Community Development Act of 1974. Before examining the nature of the criticisms against public housing, one should at the very least set forth some facts about the program.

In the first place, government ownership did produce housing. The 1949 bill established the goal of creating 810,000 units of new public housing to be built within ten years; that number of units was reached, but much more slowly than expected. The actual construction took twenty-three years. Yet it is important to recognize that the major obstacle to the construction of public housing was not the inefficiency or bureaucratic indolence of the local housing authorities. These, for the most part, were staffed by local civil servants who wanted to build more housing not only because they believed in the institution but also in the hope of increasing their chances of promotion and advancement. The slow pace usually resulted from local resistance to the construction of projects; that arose from opposition to the introduction of poor families into neighborhoods, or from resentment that the projects contributed far less than a full share of local real estate taxes. Since public housing projects were likely to include a number of black families—a number which increased during the twenty-three years following 1949—racial feelings played a significant part in the resistance to public housing, particularly in the North. Local citizens often felt that the public housing movement was intended to destroy the familiar demography of working-class neighborhoods.

Judged by two major criteria which a successful mode of housing ownership must meet, public ownership was successful. The first criterion is the ability of an ownership mode to obtain capital for construction and development. Local housing authorities obtained their capital easily, by direct borrowing in the money market. Under federal law, the obligations of these local housing authorities were tax-exempt, meaning that their buyers would not have to pay federal income taxes on the interest they received. In addition, those states which had enacted state income taxes also exempted from the state taxes interest income received on the obligations of local housing authorities located within the state.

Equally important in making the obligations of housing authorities attractive to buyers was the federal annual contributions contract, the mechanism by which the federal government met the capital costs of development. In its contract with the local housing authority, the federal government pledged to pay each year to a trustee for the bondholders the interest and amortization required by the terms of the bond indenture. This pledge was understood by bond buyers to be a solemn obligation of the United States government. In effect, then, the buyers of these bonds were getting a tax-exempt interest-bearing security which was guaranteed by the federal government, and those same buyers were willing to accept a remarkably low interest rate on this safe, tax-exempt bond. While it may be objected that the tax-exemption feature diminishes federal income tax receipts in an incalculable amount, the fact remains that this form of borrowing gave the federal government the full benefit, in the form of low interest payments, of the safety promised by the federal pledge of repayment. Other types of federal pledges have not worked so well in reducing interest rates although they are equally binding on, and expensive to, the federal government.

The second criterion of housing ownership is that it must provide continuity. A profit-making instance of private ownership provides continuity, because even if the original owners of a housing development lose interest or die, others can be expected to take their places. In contrast, ownership by local non-profit entities is not so likely to provide continuity. Usually, these agencies come into existence because a few people, sometimes even a single leader, ignite a local demand for better housing; when the leadership disperses, for whatever reason, no one can be counted on to carry on the work. No economic motive encourages substitutes to take over. Government ownership, however, does provide theoretical continuity, because, though anarchists may disagree, government appears to be one of mankind's essential institutions. Successive local administrations are impelled to conserve the assets that come into their hands, and candidates for the civil service posts in local housing authorities are as likely to appear for examinations as are prospective policemen.

None of these remarks about continuity, however, actually ensures that any specific housing authority development will enjoy the long life span of a Pyramid, or even a Sphinx. On the other hand, the failure of specific projects does not mean that the institution of ownership that developed it, and intended to maintain it, is forever doomed. Many Americans watched on television the blowing up of the notorious Pruitt-Igoe public housing project in St. Louis, and assumed that they were watching the public execution of the public housing movement for offenses against common decency. The acknowledged failure of Pruitt-Igoe, largely because its site repelled stable families, should more properly have been viewed in the perspective of the long debate over the value of public ownership of housing.

In the 1930s, when public housing started, opposition generally came from the investors in real estate and the business-minded part of the political spectrum. The liberal and labor-minded left were generally in support of the exercise of governmental power to develop and maintain housing for low-income families, though some felt the law should have explored the potential of government ownership of *contracting* as well as housing activities. Some favored direct ownership by the *federal* government rather than by authorities established by *local* governments. As the profitability of privately owned rental housing catering to low-income families has diminished over the years, so has the objection to public housing by the political right. Instead, opposition has grown in the center and left.

Some of the new opposition represents a revulsion against the "bureaucracy" which has been necessary to establish and enforce federal standards and to administer the construction subsidy system, while ensuring that the costs of local housing developments are not overstated. Actually, the process of federal underwriting of development costs in public housing has been remarkably free of scandal. The size of bureaucracy and the complexity of constructing public housing has been increased by the demands, perhaps unconscious, of some of the same groups who complain about it. This refers to the imposition of rigid environmental standards on public housing. These standards, for example, prevent the construction of new federally aided housing of *any* kind in areas characterized by high noise levels, even though local residents have been living under these conditions for years. Testing for compliance with environmental criteria and presenting environmental impact statements needed in order to qualify for federal programs now keep busy a significant part of the staff of local housing agencies and of the regional and area offices of the Department of Housing and Urban Development.

The bureaucratic growth of public housing administration has been stimulated and accelerated also by the constant addition of new items of social policy to the basic economic subsidization. Originally, the aim of public housing was merely to provide decent, safe, and sanitary homes for poor families. To this was added the insistence that the homes be provided in suitable neighborhoods. An end of racial segregation in federally subsidized housing was decreed in the 1960s. This was followed by the requirement that affirmative action programs undertake to make racially integrated housing a reality. The procedure of approving sites for public housing subsidization came to involve an elaborate method of grading them with respect to their likelihood for achieving and maintaining integrated patterns of life. The courts have been active in establishing orders of priority for admission into public housing. Courts have also participated in the establishment of procedural rules for terminating the tenancies of those already in, in the event that local authorities have found that continued residence threatened the comfort and safety of others. All of these procedures, and many more besides, have increased the requirements for staffing; this, in turn, increases the bureaucratization of public housing management, particularly in the larger cities.

Yet it is surely illusory to believe that these procedures and rules and regulations would not be invoked if the housing were to remain in private hands. The courts have already made clear that a privately owned housing development which receives significant federal subsidization is subject to the same kind of scrutiny for compliance with the law and the Constitution. Before the Housing and Community Development Act of 1974 blocked the construction of new public housing (perhaps not permanently), local authorities were embarking on so-called "turnkey" construction procedures. The plans for turnkey housing are prepared by a private developer rather than by an architect working for the authority; the private developer agrees in advance to sell the housing authority a completed development, containing a specified number of units and designed to certain agreed-upon standards. This procedure has seemed quite sensible and has helped reduce the cost of the total development, as compared with the cost of public bidding to specific plans. The turnkey process also tends to reduce the size of the authority staff.

In a similar vein, Congress authorized a public housing leasing program. This permitted local authorities to rent apartments in privately owned buildings and to sublet them to tenants eligible for admission to public housing. By acting as a buffer between the owner and the tenant, the local authority was able to ensure good housing standards, rents that tenants of low income could afford, and great flexibility as to location. This procedure also helped to reduce housing authority bureaucracy, because private owners did their own maintenance work.

Finally, Congress made it possible for housing authorities to turn over all aspects of management and maintenance of their projects to private interests on a contract basis. This, too, was an effort to reduce the size of housing authority staff and to diminish the elaborate red tape of government procedures.

None of these efforts reduced the opposition to public housing to any significant degree. As we have already noted, they were followed by an abandonment of public ownership of new housing in federal legislation in 1974, including the abandonment of the proven public housing financing method. To the criticism of the "bureaucracy" of public housing, liberal minds had over the years added the criticism that public housing "stigmatizes" the residents as being poor, that its design was stodgy and unimaginative in most cases, and that local resistance to building for the poor in middle-class areas restricted public housing to those sections which were already poor and destined all too often to be desolated.

The loss of enthusiasm for public ownership by the leftward end of the political spectrum deprived the institution of public housing of its future. No constituency to support public housing *per se* emerged. The residents in the projects have been continuously interested in asserting their rights to their own tenure; they have been quite indifferent to expanding the supply for the benefit of others. Labor unions have provided continuing support for housing measures as a whole, but since their primary objective was the employment of members in the construction of housing, the nature of its ownership was not a critical matter in their support. "Where are the friends of public housing? We never hear from them," Secretary Robert C. Weaver once remarked to a visitor who sought to rally support for larger appropriations.

But if public ownership of multiple-dwelling housing for the poor was not successful and mutual ownership, as in cooperatives or condominiums, failed to prove itself on American soil, private ownership for rent came back to public attention. In simple terms, the possibilities of private ownership can be divided into two classes, nonprofit and profit-motivated.

The advocates of nonprofit rental ownership can make a substantial case for themselves. They point to the many nonprofit institutions which play important roles in meeting basic human needs—such as voluntary hospitals and endowed colleges. They point out that many of these institutions provide housing for their staffs in supplementation of their central institutional purpose. The housing runs quite well. The same advocates then suggest that curing housing defects has become as important to the neighborhood constituencies of a city as curing disease, and that there is no reason why a community interest in housing cannot be turned to the production and maintenance of apartment houses as well as hospitals.

Unfortunately, the analogy is imperfect. Hospitals and educational institutions are run on a day-to-day basis by highly skilled professional staff; the day-to-day management of housing developments is conducted by employees of far less training and professionalism. Accordingly, unless housing nonprofit corporations grow to immense size, with more than a thousand units in occupancy, the members of their boards of directors are more likely to find themselves facing the complaints of their clients than are the members of hospital boards. In fact, the trend toward consumer protection in legislation and court action is now beginning to make itself felt even in the case of nonprofit hospital corporations, raising for their boards of directors the unpleasant specter of substantial recoveries in malpractice suits. Service ever on such boards becomes less attractive than in the past. The compensation is somewhat abstract; hospital and university still bask in a tradition of exalted public service; in both cases the board member finds himself affiliated with other serious citizens of public repute and with professional people known for their outstanding skill or scholarship. Members of the boards of both kinds of organizations share, vicariously perhaps, but nevertheless with a measure of satisfaction, the community gratitude for the great works accomplished through their help. The development of consumerist attitudes in housing, however, started earlier than in hospitals. The boards of directors of nonprofit housing agencies are not generally furnished with the companionship of men of learning, intellect, and reputation. However worthy their motives, members are likely to find themselves regarded simply as oppressors of tenants. There is, in short, no apparent satisfaction to be derived from service on a nonprofit housing corporation's board of directors, once the first thrill of completion of the new development or the rehabilitation has faded. Thus, as noted, the problem of continuity in nonprofit rental ownership is a major one indeed.

For the provision of housing for low-income families, *profit-motivated* private rental ownership also offers distinct difficulties. The major problem is not that rental ownership of social housing *must* be unprofitable; in theory massive subsidies for low-income households can make it rewarding. The source of income becomes the national government, rather than the tenants themselves. The problem posed by profit-motivated rental ownership is that so high a level of subsidization is required to place new housing units within the reach of low-income families that legislatures are reluctant to include a profit margin. Accordingly, government has devised a remarkable strategy for spreading the total subsidization under several different headings, the most important of which, from the point of view of establishing a pattern of ownership, is the Internal Revenue Code.

Under current law, the Internal Revenue Code rewards the subsidized housing builder for his patience and dexterity in managing governmental paperwork and weathering the opposition of local householders to the intrusion of unwelcome, because poorer, neighbors. The reward comes from the sale (at capital gains tax rates) of the income tax benefits which accrue to the owner-creator of a building in which the government has agreed to subsidize tenants of limited income. Tax laws are, of course, subject to change; ample notice has already been given by Congress that it dislikes the tax shelter incentive for ownership. Since it currently likes public ownership even less, however, and since it has already noted the demonstrated shortcomings of nonprofit ownership and cooperative enterprises, the tax shelter device continues and may well persist. No one can meticulously ascertain the true cost to the Treasury of housing tax shelters. To do so, one would have to ascertain what taxes would in fact be paid by the purchasers of tax shelter rights if they had not purchased them. So many other forms of tax shelter exist that such a calculation is highly conjectural.

Even if the total cost is vague, it is possible to be quite precise about the way in which the tax shelter device actually works. The Internal Revenue Code permits the owner of an apartment house to assume that it has a useful life of fifty years. The owner may therefore conclude that it loses 2 percent of its original value in each year of its life, and in consideration of that loss the owner may subtract from the annual income of the building an allowance equal to the 2 percent decline in value. If the annual depreciation allowance exceeds the net cash income of the building, no income tax need be paid on the building's income. If, indeed, the owner owns the building in his own name, or with partners, the excess depreciation will offset the taxability of the owner's *other* income from other sources. This tax benefit is obviously worth money to those taxpayers who would otherwise pay income tax on large net incomes. The builder sells a part of the ownership to such a buyer in order to realize a return on his preliminary expenses. Furthermore, if the building which produces the tax loss was constructed in order to provide government-subsidized housing for middle-income families, the Internal Revenue Code permits an even more rapid acceleration of the depreciation allowance. This provides an even greater tax offset, and is even more valuable to the purchaser.

Clearly, a building cannot be depreciated for the 100 percent; it cannot have a negative value. But in the case of social housing—housing constructed for assisted families under a government program—the Code permits what is called "double, declining balance depreciation." This schedule permits the owner to allow himself a depreciation deduction of 4 percent rather than 2 percent in the first year. In the second year, the owner is permitted 4 percent also, but the building is assumed to have depreciated to 96 percent of its value by the start of the second year. Therefore, in the second year, the actual depreciation allowance will be reduced to 3.84 percent of the original value (.96 times 4 percent). The depreciation permitted under these rules is very much greater in the first few years than the standard, so-called straight-line depreciation. To justify this, the Code provides that the owner must keep the building in operation for its original purpose—the housing of families of limited income—for at least sixteen years and eight months, or be forced to repay at least some of the forgiven taxes on the depreciation allowance. The precise amount of refund depends on the length of time the building has been occupied. Thus, the government seeks to ensure that there will be a continuity of ownership before foreclosure.

The attractiveness of a tax shelter housing investment does not depend on the operating profit of the apartment complex involved, but rather on the size of the tax loss after depreciation, in relation to the size of the cash investment by the purchasers of the shelter. If an apartment complex costs $10 million to develop and if a government-insured or a state agency-provided mortgage can be found to cover 95 percent of the total required investment, the builder will need only $500,000 of his own money to provide the equity. On the assumption that of the $10 million cost, $9 million represents buildings which are depreciable under the Code and $1 million represents land, which is not depreciable, the depreciation allowance for the first year is 4 percent of $9 million, or $360,000. If we assume that the permanent investors expect to pay 50 percent of their ordinary income as taxes, their purchase of a $360,000 tax deduction means an actual cash saving of $180,000 in the first year of ownership. In five years alone, the owners of the equity should have recovered about $800,000 in tax reductions on other income. Surely, the builder can sell the equity ownership with its attached tax shelter for considerably more than the $500,000 he put in.

The ultimate effect of this arrangement may well be to promote economic activity in spheres *other* than housing. By offsetting ordinary income earned in any fully taxable way— such as playing professional basketball—the tax shelter element of the housing subsidy program encourages those who play professionally to demand high salaries. In order to pay them, the owners of basketball teams build, or demand that their cities build, bigger stadiums, which, incidentally, consume materials, labor, and land that might otherwise be used for housing.

The income tax shelter represents only one of the costs of housing subsidization which might otherwise offer an unsolvable political problem. We must also consider the cost to local governments of the total exemption from, or the substantial reduction of, real property taxes. This exemption or reduction must usually be authorized in order to keep the rents within the range of families who require assistance. Spreading part of the cost between federal and local government naturally reduces the amount of outright subsidization which the federal government would otherwise be required to adopt through the legislative process. Local real estate tax exemption or abatement is a much less obvious form of indirect subsidization, but it is provided by local government, which cannot really afford it. We should also note that the savings produced by a tax shelter in housing require a very substantial mortgage to make it attractive. The normal mortgage institutions are not prepared to make such loans without federal assistance in the form of mortgage insurance. Here again, a more subtle form of federal assistance is required, including the provision of funds with which the Government National Mortgage Association can purchase these long-term, partially subsidized, relatively low interest rate mortgages from the banks which are willing to originate them, but not to hold them for their fifty-year term while general interest rates might rise.

This complex set of what might be called subterfuges—direct subsidies in the form of massive federal rent- or mortgage-interest-reduction payments added to income tax subsidies added to local real property tax subsidies—are not the product of a devious mind running amok. On the contrary, this layer cake of complementary subsidies was baked over the years since 1960 by congressmen and administration leaders who seriously wanted to utilize a more nearly adequate share of national resources to provide a present in the form of better homes for low-income families in the cities. The practical difficulties of private entrepreneurship in the field of housing the poor are so onerous and the enterprise itself is so unprofitable that one must provide massive help if private ownership of social housing is to be maintained. It is the political difficulty of providing so high a level of subsidy which ordains its indirection.

Even with the subsidies, significant money stakes are put up by the developer of subsidized housing at the very beginning. Land must be acquired; sometimes its present occupants must be relocated. Architectural drawings may cost as much as $300,000 to $400,000 for a development of a thousand units of high-rise construction. Then there are legal fees, followed by fees for engineering, for research on foundations, for the preparation of environmental statements, for fair market renting or cooperative sales plans, for advice on community relations. Liability for all of these must be incurred before approval can be obtained for mortgage insurance, or a state housing agency mortgage commitment issued. In a project which actually proceeds, a large part, if not all, of these advance costs will be refunded from the mortgage proceeds. But if the project is for any reason derailed before the actual start of construction or, perhaps, before its completion, most of the money spent in preliminaries will have been lost.

Above all, the developer must devote large amounts of his *time* to initiating a project. Time is the basic resource of anyone engaged in the development business. The aspect of development which consumes the largest amount of time is the acquisition of the land needed for a housing project. To assist in this respect, government may offer the use of its power of eminent domain to acquire land for privately owned social housing, and may even, in what's left of the urban renewal program, sell the acquired land at whatever price below its original acquisition cost will assure the economic feasibility of the social housing plan.

Since these stimulants are always administered with depressants in the form of a limitation on operating profits (as contrasted with tax shelter sale profits), the state of New York feared that developers might be unwilling to take them. This, of course, would mean an end to new or rehabilitated privately owned social housing in that state. At a time when none dared admit that a solution to every social problem did not sit in waiting, requiring only to be called on like a hotel bellhop, this fear produced a government agency which was authorized to discharge all of the private entrepreneur's tedious obligations. The Urban Development Corporation, as it was called, was prepared to sell the completed housing development back into private hands, earning a presumed profit for the state.

Armed with formidable public powers, including the power to borrow money on general obligations and thus to act as its own mortgage banker, the UDC was presided over by Edward J. Logue, one of the most energetic and imaginative of all the urban redevelopers of the postwar period. Under his leadership, the UDC was able to borrow money from the bond-buying public and use it for land acquisition, architectural and engineering studies, market research, and ultimately for housing and even for industrial construction in the state. (Federal laws on local government tax exemption limited the portion of UDC funds which could go into industrial development.) The ability of the UDC to borrow money on its *general* obligations gave it a sense of immunity from market tests of individual projects which would have needed individual mortgages, luring its socially committed leaders into deeper and deeper waters. The bottom disappeared in 1973, when the Nixon administration called a "moratorium" on the use of funds for mortgage-interest reduction, otherwise known as the FHA 236 program, which provided the interest-cost subsidy which is the basic building block of privately owned social housing.

Nevertheless, the UDC continued to start more projects, and was able to borrow money as late as the fall of 1974, when suddenly someone discovered that the prospective revenues, including both occupants' rentals and federal subsidies, were insufficient to cover the debt service on money that had already been borrowed, or that remained still to be borrowed if incomplete projects were to be finished. The resulting squeeze stimulated a reappraisal of all borrowing by local government, particularly in the state of New York, which nearly carried the city of New York into insolvency. One almost certain result—if anything in this field can be certain—is that no further experiments in publicly owned private development agencies will be financed. This leaves the ownership of social housing, under present legislation, in the hands of private investors, who will choose this use of their funds only because they care about tax benefits, not because they care about the ultimate value of the housing itself.

This finally raises the central issue about ownership. Is the private ownership of social housing so important as to justify the difficulties of devising an alternative to public ownership with heavy public subsidies? The requirement for equity under most of the effective mortgage schemes in this field is now less than 10 percent of the development cost. Why should the federal and local governments have had to develop so complicated a scheme to lure so small a part of the total capital? Might it not be wiser to use the private interests simply as contractors, building for direct government ownership the housing that none wishes to own for its investment value? By analogy, the present program resembles a privately owned American navy that is supported by government-owned shipyards and munitions plants.

When the truly persistent questioner begins to understand that more than 90 percent of the costs of social housing are provided by the government through an elaborate system of mortgage credit and the subsidy layer cake, the ironies in the current American rejection of the public ownership of housing become all the more striking. If government is by far the majority investor in the new, subsidized apartment houses, why should it not logically be the owner?

2

RESOURCES
FOR THE FUTURE

Determining modes of ownership and tenure to fit the several needs of social housing is merely the first step in developing a national housing policy. It must be followed by an accounting of the pertinent resources and a strategy for marshaling them to best advantage. Resources for housing can be classified conveniently under five headings:

First, existing housing. To the extent that the existing stockpile is satisfactory, it eliminates the need for demolition and conserves other resources. To the extent that it is unsatisfactory but reclaimable, it may itself supply the basic resource for improvement. To the extent that it is beyond economic reclamation, it constitutes only an apparent asset; in reality, it is an obstacle to be overcome. What is worse, existing housing provides a ready rallying point for those who oppose the use of national resources to help the underhoused. Housing policy must draw these distinctions.

Second, land. New housing can be constructed only if satisfactory locations can be found for it. Our definition of housing as one bundle of three packages—the utility, the social, and the shelter packages—tells us that the national investment is minimized when new housing can be built in existing communities. Naturally, the desire for economy must be weighed against the danger of adding to the load on facilities that are overutilized, obsolescent, politically unadaptable to the needs of the prospective new residents, or irrelevant to employment, industrial or commercial trends.

Third, building materials and technology. All over the world, the design of housing reflects prevailing local climatic conditions and the availability of raw materials. The highly industrialized, homogenized national economy of the United States does not obliterate *all* regional differences in housing types; builders and designers take some account of local variations in the availability of specific raw materials. Nonetheless, American technology has tended to produce a national standard of housing expectations. This imposes a demand for architectural designs that are sometimes inappropriate for particular locations and may involve the use of materials more expensive than those in local abundance.

Fourth, a pool of labor capable of constructing housing on site, manufacturing its components off site and providing the necessary transportation. Despite many technological changes introduced over the past half century and an apparent growing dependence on factory-made and partially preassembled components, the housing product continues to require a rich infusion of local labor. This has complicated the development of industrial unionism; the several crafts involved have maintained their separate identities, and the local unions within the craft internationals have sustained their own rules for apprenticeship and admission of members.

The courts have intervened to widen the labor pool and to eliminate racial and hereditary barriers to union membership. But the local unions may well have a certain practical justice on their side when they limit boom-time membership expansion in recollection of the cyclical ups and downs of the past. At the very least, the maintenance of a consistently high level of activity in similar fields (hospital and school construction, for example) is probably essential to the supply of an adequate labor force for housing.

Fifth, economic development. The economy must be able to provide the goods and services demanded by those who work in the construction and related trades. The housing industry makes a long-lived product that is not immediately valuable in satisfying the consumer desires of the work force, and there are limits to labor's willingness to sacrifice consumption goods for the production of capital goods, as even the directors of socialist economies have found. Hence a healthy credit market is essential to housing development.

Many housing programs have foundered because the nature and use of these resources were insufficiently understood, and the resulting ill-conceived strategies inevitably misfired. Before proceeding further, then, we should examine each of the resources for housing in greater detail.

EXISTING HOUSING

Perhaps the easiest of all housing resources to misunderstand is buildings already standing. The demolition of these structures seems clearly wasteful, not only of physical assets but of human and community relationships. Making inadequate homes more nearly habitable would appear to obviate the need to relocate people and would keep that twentieth-century monster, the bulldozer, locked in its garage.

With the passing of its initial enthusiasm for slum clearance, the federal government has increasingly given preference to the reuse of existing housing. Special mortgage-interest subsidies have been offered for rehabilitation in urban renewal areas (the FHA 312 program), and public housing authorities have been allowed to rent and sublet renovated buildings. State and local laws have also been extended to provide mortgage loans for upgrading purposes as well as for new construction. New York, in particular, has led the way by authorizing municipal loans for the renewal of multiple dwellings and by encouraging the installation of central heating and modern plumbing and electrical systems through special tax breaks. But dissimilarities in the type and condition of buidings occupied in urban America have made it difficult to formulate a uniform national rehabilitation scheme.

The six-story tenement house of Manhattan's Lower East Side, where the density of development reflected the high land value of the 1870s and 1880s, is not found in most other cities. In Boston and Chicago, the poor have typically been housed in wood-frame "four-flatters." The low-income populations of Philadelphia, Wilmington, and Baltimore have traditionally occupied small, single-family brick row houses.

In addition, whole sections of large Northern cities built for the middle or upper classes have been taken over by the poor. And the flight of the original occupants to the suburbs has been followed by a gross disintegration of the social package, which has in turn discouraged new investment in the shelter itself. Policy makers must decide how, if at all, new resources can be put into the old structures to maintain them in comparative decency.

It has been argued that the automobile offers a paradigm for American housing: In its primal state, the automobile gives its original purchaser high-quality transportation, but it continues to provide satisfactory service to subsequent owners of successively lesser means, presumably at correspondingly lower cost, until eventually the expense of repair exceeds any possible residual usefulness for transportation and the car is junked. This model reproduces faithfully the course of the one-family house except for the crucial fact that the market value of a private home drops when its neighborhood deteriorates, while a car has no neighborhood.

Moreover, as a house shifts to lower-income ownership, covering its basic costs will very likely make overcrowding inevitable. Overcrowding itself will increase the costs of maintenance, while the increased population will make the neighborhood appear less stable to the bank that might be asked to renew or extend a mortgage. FHA home-modernization loan insurance represents a governmental response to the threat of one-family home decay, but the scope of the problem of neighborhood decline far exceeds any single institutional remedy.

If the used-car analogy only approximately describes the economics of the one-family house, it is less applicable to the multiple dwelling that filters down through the hands of less and less affluent tenants. The competitive interests of owner and occupant discourage fresh investment in older properties: Why, says the owner, should I risk *my* money for *their* benefit? Those who design public policy must devise ways to maintain the landlord's concern for the relatively long-term soundness of his property. Unfortunately, this concern frequently dissolves into panic with the changing demography of a neighborhood.

Frightened by what he sees taking place, the owner caught in the population shift begins looking for a buyer. Most likely, he will have to settle on someone with precisely the point of view antithetic to social policy—that is, he can find only someone who does not care about long-range prosperity, and does not balk at the high cost of good maintenance of land property because he intends not to provide good maintenance. This buyer, eager for the quick dollar, will aim for a high weekly or monthly income and ignore the consequent deterioration of his building. (Lower maintenance standards, many writers on housing have concluded, may be the only rational economic response to a drop in the income level of tenants.)

The new buyer is in any case discouraged from adopting a long-range perspective by the refusal of most banks to increase mortgages in an area where they perceive the kind of social change that they interpret as presaging the arrival of short-range owners. Government tries to interrupt decay by imposing a higher level of maintenance expenditure through housing code inspections followed by fines for noncompliance. This police action tends to discourage ownership and too often leads to more rapid disinvestment and abandonment.

If the marketplace is to keep up the standards of older multiple dwellings, the government must somehow bring about bank loans for repairs and rehabilitation in sagging neighborhoods. New York, so far without visible results or a fair test of the risk involved, is experimenting with a program that will partially insure bank loans for building improvements in areas that are slipping but have not fallen altogether. Other cities have begun to use Federal Community Development Grants for this purpose. Obviously much more than the present total amount of federal funds available will be needed to do the job.

Government intervention of another kind is essential in neighborhoods where incomes are simply too low to support the level of rent necessary to meet a building's operating and capital expenses. Experience has shown, however, that public assistance payments to sustain family income do not of themselves improve the quality of housing. Rental grants must be accompanied by the subsidization of rehabilitation plus—and this is perhaps most important—a sound management program for the renovated building. And sound management requires the freedom to purge (admittedly a horrid word) the destructive tenant.

Similarly, sound public policy for arresting or restoring the deterioration of multifamily housing must include provision for bringing a realistic threat to bear against both the owner and the occupants. Theoretically, the market takes care of this: The landlord knows that if he allows his building to deteriorate too badly, he will be able to attract only the least desirable tenants; the destructive tenant faces the prospect of being forced to move to less desirable quarters. Though such an idealized market probably has never existed because of the stickiness of housing as a commodity—its relentless adherence to land narrows the lessor's choices—government efforts to approximate the sanctions are quite instructive.

The available penalties for an owner who fails to maintain his building in accordance with the law are either too mild, and have little deterrent value, or too severe, and deter reinvestment more effectively than they encourage compliance with the housing codes. As for the regulations against unruly tenants, they are virtually unenforceable. Peer-group pressure is unquestionably the most effective sanction.

This brings us to the task of promoting high expectations for neighborhoods under renewal. Since this task falls into the sphere of public relations and political promises, officials have pursued it assiduously, designating neighborhood development plans, neighborhood preservation districts, neighborhood conservation districts, and the like. Sometimes, even with little or no direct government intercession, certain areas succeed in "trickling upward" from low .rent to high-rent occupancy (presenting horrendous problems, it should be realized, for the people displaced in the process). But most of the flow is in the opposite direction, which means that the crucial question is how to improve a neighborhood without uprooting the nondestructive majority who live there.

All rescue plans have depended primarily on providing money for rehabilitation. So-called "moderate" rehabilitation leaves the interior partition walls and room arrangements as they were, and seeks merely to restore the building to minimum habitability by replacing fallen plaster, eliminating infestation, and repairing the plumbing, heating, and electrical systems. Or the process may involve stripping an old building to its skeleton and starting anew from there. In both cases, a high rate of failure of buildings *after* rehabilitation indicates that new investment capital is not enough to breathe life into substandard housing.

The real difficulty in resuscitating an older building begins after the plasterers and painters have departed, when the manager selects his new tenants. For the hard truth is that some people are incapable of meeting minimum standards of housekeeping or neighborly behavior, and the presence of any considerable percentage of unruly residents in an apartment house makes it unacceptable to other residents.

Most rehabilitated multifamily buildings are too small to

justify the cost of efficient full-time superintendent and janitorial services. In the structure with four or fewer units, a resident owner can be expected to handle much of the repair and maintenance work himself. But this leaves the question of who or what is to replace the janitor's wife in the typical twenty-four-unit apartment house.

Many have suggested that a wholly new form of enterprise is needed, directed by young people with a demonstrated emotional commitment to the improvement of living conditions for low-income families in the central city and possessing as well a practical sense of how to get things done. Such enterprises might fill the gap, if they could be made to work. But initial funding would have to be provided on a scale that private foundations are unprepared to meet, and the possibility of a large and embarrassing failure deters government agencies from trying to find ways around current legislative and constitutional prohibitions against making grants of public funds to private persons.

While the idea seems promising, few experiments in nonprofit ownership that have actually been tried have yet become fully self-supporting. The costs of providing management and maintenance services are not reduced very much by the elimination of the need to show a profit. A nonprofit entity will therefore continue to need subsidies if it is to provide necessary services. Even with operating subsidies, it is unlikely that the buildings involved will ever enjoy a rent roll large enough to sustain management quality matching that of the better public housing agencies. Still, the emerging social institutions of the urban ghettos—groups like the Housing Development Corporation of the New York City Council of Churches—are determined to provide these services and in special cases, when they choose their customers with care, they may succeed.

In addition to providing technical services, the management of an apartment house requires the exercise of judgment to distinguish between those for whom a touch of patience will be highly productive and those who merely will take advantage of any sign of weakness to live free of rent. Sometimes these discriminating talents are possessed uniquely by a single resident, sometimes jointly by a small leadership group capable of eliciting tenant discipline to minimize wear and tear in the rehabilitated building. The Upper Park Avenue Community Association of Manhattan is an outstanding example of the good work of a small leadership group.

To use existing housing creatively, public policy must indicate how to duplicate achievements that depend on the ability of talented leaders to deal face to face with tenants. Too often, these very qualities disappear or lie unused when the government seeks to increase the size of a successful enterprise; the proven gifts of the original leaders are shelved, while they try, with uncertain results, to become administrators on a larger scale.

For all these reasons, then, the nation's older urban buildings remain an ambiguous resource for improving the housing supply. To the extent that the social package surrounding and permeating old buildings can be repaired and strengthened, they become highly valuable; to the extent that the social fabric remains torn beyond mending by any of the means currently available to housing policy makers (social work, anti-narcotics therapy, and, above all, the dignifying gift of productive and amply paid work), existing substandard housing probably constitutes a dubious or even a negative asset.

It is easier to start from nothing, to build in what has been a wheat field, than to reconstruct the physical matrix that holds the survivors of hard-core poverty and intense racial discrimination. This perception, though not always consciously recognized, probably makes the notion of wholly New Towns so attractive to many dedicated improvers of the species. Convinced that the existing social package cannot be repaired at any price, these idealists are prepared to assume the financial cost of creating a very costly new utility package to escape the inner-city quagmire.

LAND

If the value of America's existing deteriorated and dilapidated housing is ambiguous, that of its land is even more so. Certainly the land is there. In relation to its total population, the United States enjoys an abundance of land practically unheard of in any other industrialized nation. Over the country as a whole—not necessarily the most relevant way to gauge the scope of useful resources—the general population density is about 56 people to the square mile. This is roughly one fourth the density of France, one tenth that of the United Kingdom, and one fifteenth that of Belgium. Even in comparison with the nonindustrialized world, the United States is remarkably well favored in land per person. The vast expanse of Asia, for example, has more than three times as many people per square mile.

The history of civilization is, in one sense, the record of increasing intensity of land use. Farming and herding produced a greater quantity of edible food per acre than did hunting; gathering previously dispersed cottage workers into factories greatly enhanced the potential of industrialization, once a means had been found to tap manufacturing energy from sources other than men and their beasts. The concentration of factories and special services that makes high-level production possible has, of course, resulted in the agglomeration of people in cities.

In the second and third quarters of this century, a remarkably flexible, if expensive, transportation system has developed in the industrial countries. The public highway and the private automobile have extended the span of useful land around the central cities. Housing, industry, and commerce have been able to spread into areas that were formerly suitable for farming alone.

Accessibility—vastly expanded with the help of highway trust funds, railroad subsidies, and the consequent dedication of acreage to transport purposes—has led to a striking increase in the value of suburban property. Indeed, the locational value of land (supported by public investment and a measure of private intervention) has risen until it is worth far more as a platform for housing than as soil for crops. The prospect of inheritance taxes on the illiquid capital value of the land, combined with higher property taxes (sometimes diminished by special agricultural concessions to preserve open space), has accelerated the shift from agriculture to housing.

The intensified use of outlying land for housing has been accompanied by a reduction in the residential density of inner-city land. Though the number of households is not declining, America's central cities are losing population steadily. A trick of political boundary drawing often conceals the full impact of the trend. To take an outstanding case, New York City—as a whole—remained practically constant in population between the 1960 and the 1970 Census. But this broad statement conceals the fact that the city swallowed a large part of its suburbs when it incorporated Queens, Brooklyn, the upper Bronx, and Staten Island in 1898. If an observer narrowed his focus to Manhattan and the lower Bronx, which together constituted the original New York, he would find that its population declined in the sixties as it had steadily from its peak in 1910.

Manhattan's present population also differs significantly from that of only thirty years ago. By 1970, its public school population had become 75 percent nonwhite. If New York as a whole had been confined to its 1898 boundaries, everyone would recognize it to be as markedly nonwhite as Newark has become.

Over the years reformers have directed their most persistent criticisms of urban slum housing against the effects of high density. High density means correspondingly little open space; it limits the play of sunlight in the windows of living rooms, impedes the circulation of air, degrades all of the sanitary facilities, promotes the spread of disease, and, perhaps most significant, cheats families of their sense of privacy and undermines their belief in their own importance and potentialities. Many of these defects have been cured by means other than the reduction of density; public health advances, for example, have made moot the argument that crowded living conditions encourage the spread of bacterial disease. Tuberculosis, cholera, yellow fever, and diphtheria no longer take a regular toll of America's urban poor as they did a century ago.

The outcry against high housing density has softened, too, with the growing awareness that propinquity to others is an urban value treasured by at least part of the population. The concentration of minority group members in close physical proximity is also seen as a source of political power, enabling them to elect local representatives, something they could not do if their numbers were dispersed over a wider geographical area.

Nevertheless, the majority of Americans would undoubtedly express a preference for low-density housing development. Local zoning ordinances legitimize widespread opposition to high-rise apartment houses or multiple dwellings. Residents often take action scarcely stopping at the threshold of violence to prevent increases in the housing density of their neighborhoods or political communities. Thus our inquiry into the usefulness of the land resource for improving housing conditions for the poor divides into two interlocking questions. How can the resisting suburbs be made to accept a larger population, consisting in part of lower-income people who now live in the most crowded and deteriorating neighborhoods? What does the migration outward offer the city and its poor—will it enlarge or diminish their power to achieve better housing?

The battle against suburban exclusivity and the struggle to loosen the middle-class "noose," usually white, that threatens to strangle the central city were causes whose ultimate virtue was taken for granted by progressive Americans until a few years ago. But the recent surge of interest in the environment, coupled with the wave of despondence that followed the initial victories of the civil rights movement, has made many people more sympathetic to the suburban point of view. If, as it now appears, a sense of ownership is actually important to good housing maintenance, and if pride is an important ingredient in the sense of ownership, then it follows that the suburbanite's concern about neighborhood values, about moderate densities that do not strain the natural resources of an area, about excess traffic and the environmental impact of too much development, cannot simply be dismissed as snobbish determination to keep out strangers, particularly those with less money and, perhaps, a different religion or skin color.

In many cases, to be sure, the suburbanite's concern with environmental quality contains elements (and often crucial elements) of class pride and racial prejudice. Yet it cannot wholly be dismissed as the product of unworthy motives. For perhaps the first time in American history, the value of growth itself has become subject to legitimate debate. Unfortunately, the effort to discriminate between the growth that fulfills human needs and the growth that thwarts them is in danger of sinking in a flood of mutual recriminations between advocates of limiting development and those who feel the suggested limits are often intended to keep the poor and nonwhite in the central city. This, whether intentional or not, would be the inevitable consequence of severely restricted suburban development.

Meanwhile, Congress has responded to rising fears about the quality of the environment by adopting the National Environmental Policy Act, and the courts have handed down a long list of decisions affecting land use under the terms of the act. The legislation, as applied by HUD, has had the effect of reducing the amount of land available for the construction of social housing. Meeting environmental criteria also makes housing more expensive to build and operate on sites on which federal rules apply—where mortgage insurance or subsidies are to be used.

Among other things, the National Environmental Policy Act discourages the use of land that subjects it to environmental influences deemed adverse to human health and comfort. For instance, urban locations are excluded from federal subsidy benefits if they are afflicted by traffic noise during more than a certain number of hours per day. If the decibel level exceeds the standards only moderately the site falls into a doubtful category. In that case, HUD may prescribe remedial measures to bring it into the acceptable range. The remedies frequently include double-paned windows, expensive to install and to replace when somebody throws a baseball through them, and air conditioning—which, besides being expensive, obviously adds to energy consumption. Though the solution may thereby contribute to other environmental problems, these fall into the lap of a different federal agency.

Anyone who spends time watching HUD in its cumbersome weighing of potential environmental shortcomings and their remedies will soon conclude that the department is far more cautious in its appraisal of these matters when it thinks its decision may be challenged by a party inimical to the construction of housing. Should, unhappily, the combination of environmental defects and possible opposition move HUD to demand not merely an environmental fact sheet but a full environmental impact statement, the housing project under consideration will probably be delayed at least a year, with a consequent inflationary escalation of its basic costs as well as the imposed added expense of installing internal environmental protection devices. After having contended with the issues arising from sanitary sewer loads, school population patterns, and transportation load factors, the supporter of social housing programs may be forgiven for suspecting that the environmental movement has been conceived primarily to prevent the construction of housing for those who need it most.

An even greater confusion descends on the housing sympathizer who attempts to forge from the decisions of the federal and state courts a consistent land use policy. In some jurisdictions, local townships have been upheld in "zoning out" projects that might produce low-income housing at moderate densities. The courts have noted that the towns have not provided adequate sewers and sewage treatment plants for the increasing population and, in reality, rewarded their neglect by restraining the growth the majority did not want. The local government therefore continues to fail to install these facilities in the happy knowledge that so long as it refuses to spend tax money on sanitation, it need not fear the arrival of unwelcome neighbors.

Other courts in the same state have taken diametrically the opposite point of view, ruling that the zoning restriction against moderate-density housing, or low-rise multiple dwellings, was not a reasonable protection of the environment. Instead, the restrictive zoning was construed as an effort to limit the constitutional right of other Americans to live where they choose. One court undertook to provide equitable relief by establishing its own zoning pattern for the offending town, with the help of professional consultants.

A leading case on the rights of suburban townships to limit growth emerged from a plan devised by the town of Ramapo, New York, to prevent "premature" development within its boundaries. New construction was made conditional on the installation by the town of necessary public improvements scheduled over a long period of years. But the zoning ordinance provides that if the town fails to complete the improvements on schedule a developer may undertake them at his own expense and claim tax credit for the cost. In this way a balance was struck between the need of land for housing purposes and the rights of the present townspeople to protect themselves against the deterioration that might follow unwise development. The Ramapo ordinance was upheld by the New York State Court of Appeals, the highest court in the state.

The current uncertainty regarding the availability of suburban land for housing people from the cities, particularly those of low income, reflects the unsettled conflict of interest between those who already live in the suburbs and those who want to move there. Local control of land use, subject only to rather cursory review—usually confined to procedural questions—is the general rule in the United States. Appeal of local actions on substantive grounds has been almost impossible in the past, although the courts are beginning to move in this direction. In the absence of a national policy to guide the allocation of land for social housing and serve as a basis for judicial review of local decisions, land availability will be determined less by regional considerations than by uncoordinated private efforts. Many varied organizations throughout the country will continue their separate campaigns to "bust" local zoning and free space for the urban population to live in imitation of the suburban dweller.

In June 1974, Congress failed to pass a National Land Use Policy Act by a mere seven votes. While it would have helped to meet the financial problems of land use planning, its bureaucratic overtones were acutely heard by those who generally oppose federal intervention in local affairs. The New York *Daily News*, for example, in an editorial applauding the bill's defeat, said local officials who accepted such federal grants would wake up to find that "a corps of bossy, brassy, we-know-what's-best-for-everyone bureaucrats is running around braying orders. . . . Once that starts, home rule and private property rights would be trampled into oblivion."

Not long ago, most progressives would have disagreed with that view in every respect, but recently there has been an increasing fear of government size and uncontrollability, and a growing insistence on the priority of the individual over the institution. By the same token, many erstwhile supporters of public housing have, so to speak, rediscovered the value of individual ownership. Still, progressives of all persuasions— those most strongly in favor of more land for low-income housing as well as those more concerned about preserving natural resources and open space—are agreed on the need for a national land use policy, even if they remain widely divided on what that policy should be.

In a country as heterogeneous as the United States, local zoning control offers a way of preserving a comforting degree of homogeneity. Since most people combine, in one proportion or another, a taste for neighborhood cohesiveness with a taste for the spice of variety, agreement on what constitutes a judicious balance will be difficult to reach. In the meantime, the question of how much land is realistically available for the needs of social housing will be left without a general answer; tentative *ad hoc* settlements will be worked out in widely separated locales, such as New York's Forest Hills and California's oceanfront.

MATERIALS AND TECHNOLOGY

The natural resources of any nation shape its architectural tastes, particularly in housing. The United States is, like Finland, especially rich in forest resources, and lumber has consequently become a preferred building material in both countries. It has the virtue of being self-regenerating, provided that men harvest it with restraint. At any one time and in any specific region, though, it may be available only in limited quantities. These limits are frequently approached or exceeded when housing production rises.

Since most of America's one- and two-family homes are constructed predominantly of lumber, its price usually moves in phase with the demand for housing. In 1973, when the production of new housing units peaked at about 2.6 million, lumber costs rose to all-time highs. Even so, as building materials go, wood is not only comparatively cheap, but unusually versatile and easy to work with. American technology long ago became adept at exploiting it. For example, the invention of the balloon-framed house—based on the theory that two-by-four pine studding is sufficiently rigid to frame a building two stories high—was a crucial American contribution to architecture.

European practice—except in the northern parts of Scandinavia, where softwood forests exist on a scale commensurate with those originally found in America—has emphasized clay, stone, and mortar construction in housing. It would probably be economically advantageous if local styles everywhere could vary from year to year with the ebb and flow of market demands, but the habits of a locality defy this adaptability. Because European materials are heavier, not self-regenerating, and require heat and chemical reactions to make them useful, as in the case of brick and mortar, the cost of construction there tends to be material-intensive, whereas in the United States it has generally been labor-intensive.

The American pattern has been emphasized by the local organization of the buiding-trades unions. Yet it is a curious fact that much of the lower-skilled construction labor all around the world has been monopolized by nonindigenous people—the Algerians in France, the Turks in Scandinavia, the Arabs in Israel, and, typically, Irish and Italian immigrants in the United States. The Italians on the eastern seaboard have been described as starting out on these shores carrying mortar in a hod and becoming contractors as soon as they could afford a wheelbarrow.

The connection between local labor, regional fashion or habit, and the choice of materials used in construction has been codified in the building and construction laws. These standards are set primarily by local governments, although strenuous efforts have been made by state governments, professional associations, and HUD to supersede local ordinances with more nearly universal requirements. The building codes do serve to protect the public from the danger of shoddy, fire-prone structures. But they have undeniably been tainted by their local connection with contractors who believe that competition can be controlled or minimized by mandating the use of specific materials and subassemblies. The unions, too, are notoriously interested in assuring their workers an accustomed minimum of man-hours for work that, as a matter of law, cannot be eliminated or simplified.

While resistance to innovative materials and methods is anathema to all the paladins of virtue, there is reason to question whether the specification codes are as rigid as they are generally represented to be. As for the union involvement, according to some estimates as much as 60 percent of all housing built in the United States is nonunion.

Furthermore, the unions have accepted a long list of new materials and techniques in the years since World War II. Productivity has increased markedly and, at least until 1965, the index of housing construction costs in this country rose little or no faster than the index of family income.

Even in the high-cost housing areas of the nation (identified by HUD), the price of postwar construction was held down by the introduction of reinforced concrete in place of steel, the substitution of precast or prestressed concrete wall sections for brick, and the use of prefabricated gypsum board sections for partition walls instead of job-assembled wooden studs, lathing, and three coats of field-installed plaster. Some unions, of course, have been more receptive than others to labor-saving or material-cost-saving types of assembly, but the trend toward revised work rules is unmistakable. True, it has been accompanied by another trend: higher hourly wages and greater fringe benefits. And the rigid division of trades continues—making small complex jobs, like housing rehabilitation, economically unfeasible under present building-trades conditions. However, in 1976, a giant step forward was taken by the major international unions, which agreed to cut the number of trades required in rehabilitation to four, eliminating tremendously expensive overlapping functions. The question which remains is whether the local trade unions will go along with this policy. As in the case of other unions, the organization of the building trades does not permit the internationals to dictate policy to their locals.

The savings afforded by new materials and technological advances in the 1960s were wiped out not only by rising labor costs but also by a rising view of what should be included in a house. The standard single-family tract house sold in the mid-seventies at, say, $30,000 is four times as expensive as the one offered to families in the same stratum of the income pyramid thirty years ago by Levitt & Sons. The structural differences are probably not very great, yet the mechanical and electrical changes, the inventory of what must now be provided to make a kitchen acceptable—the type of range, refrigerator, dishwasher, etc.—plus the automatically controlled heating system and a host of plumbing conveniences have all added enormously to the final price. Similarly, the movement to high-rise construction in the central cities, stimulated by the increased cost of land assemblage and acquisition, necessitates complex mechanical and electrical systems that push up rent levels.

Nor does this end the matter. The basic raw materials of the traditional American home—lumber, sand, clay for bricks, asbestos for roofing shingle and Transite piping, to name only a few—have become more expensive as sources convenient to construction sites have been exhausted and as environmental interests have imposed conservation measures on the extractors. Some of the manufacturing processes involved, like the calcining and the pulverization of portland cement, produce smoke and dust in great volume; where the cost of controlling the polluting effluent exceeds the value of an existing plant, it may have to be closed down for environmental considerations, reducing supply. Even if the supply is later augmented by the construction of a new plant, the cost of the requisite environmental controls will not be offset by the economies of modern technology, and the unit cost of the product will have to go up.

Other building materials—notably copper vital to noncorrosive piping and bauxite for making aluminum—are derived from overseas sources. Their prices have risen significantly in recent years and undoubtedly will continue to do so. This will increase pressures for more reviews of existing building and mechanical codes in the hope that changes in permissible materials may reduce American housing dependence on high-cost overseas sources.

There has already been much talk about the virtues of "performance codes" that stipulate, for instance, the number of hours of fire resistance a certain wall installation must be capable of, as an alternative to the traditional "specification codes" that require the wall to be built of bricks or concrete block of a given thickness laid up in mortar of a given composition. Unfortunately, it is extremely hard to make a performance code work. Who can tell whether a proposed type of fire wall will indeed resist for four hours? Who should test it? Must each city establish its own laboratory? Who will decide whether the test conditions are realistic?

These questions are continually raised by professional engineers and architects who fear that changes in standards will undermine their own established ability to interpret the code, or otherwise adversely affect their livelihood. Flexible copper tubing would appear to be a cheap, corrosion-free substitute for rigid brass piping that must be threaded and pieced together on the construction site. Plastic tubing would appear to be an even cheaper substitute for copper tubing. Yet many American cities have been prevented from approving these materials by opponents who base their rationale on the difficulty of stipulating in the building code exactly how such components are to be installed and the lack of field experience to determine how satisfactory they may be.

In addition to looking for new low-cost materials, housing economists have long advocated a total "systems approach" to factory-built housing. In what he called "Operation Breakthrough," former HUD Secretary George Romney conducted a competition to qualify as "promising" a number of different prefabricated housing schemes. Since the Breakthrough projects were to be erected in cities with detailed building codes, there could be no significant deviation from normal construction standards. Unlike mobile-home manufacturers, the participating firms could not trim costs by reducing, say, the size of the wooden scantlings in the walls.

As Romney was soon to learn, there is no economy in the centralized mass production of housing, or anything else for that matter, unless it can be carried on at a very high volume, which requires a large ready market. The more expensive the product, the more difficult it is to construct the market. Just as the mass production of automobiles was scarcely feasible before a network of suitable roads had been built, so mass prefabrication of housing is economically unpromising until sufficient sites become available for it. And the issue of land, of course, remains a local matter, twisting in the winds of local politics.

Even assuming that sufficient volume could be achieved, there may be no intrinsic savings in factory systems specifically designed to build housing. The units may be too big to transport and production schedules may be too inflexible, since economic pressures would force plants to commit their capacity far in advance, severely limiting their adaptability to the sudden expansion and contraction characteristic of the American construction industry.

In sum, there is no technological breakthrough in sight that will stop the steady upward curve of construction prices. Consequently, moderate-cost housing for the poor will become ever more difficult to achieve. Though we should not abandon efforts to develop more efficient materials and assemblies, it seems likely that economies will be gained only by cutting back on amenities. Given the built-in reasons why all producers want to make a more, not a less elaborate house, a movement downward, wise as it might appear after long research, would be politically acceptable to the producers only if it carried a clear promise of a high volume of future work. An effort to persuade the poor to settle for a significantly lower standard would have to be coupled with a restraining force to cut back on the quality of housing amenity still flaunted by the very rich.

LABOR

According to the U.S. Department of Labor, approximately 1.25 million new employees would have to enter the building trades for the nation to meet all the anticipated construction goals of the 1970s. Of these, perhaps 500,000 would be needed for housing purposes, an addition of about 16 percent to the work force of about 3 million Americans engaged in on-site housing construction last year. With the overall unemployment rate in 1976 exceeding 8 percent, there would seem to be no danger of a manpower shortage.

Yet on-site construction represents only a part of the total labor requirement for housing. Materials must be prepared and transported, tools must be manufactured, and future trends in these fields remain obscure. Environmental considerations may make the extracting and processing of building materials more labor-intensive and cause them to be shipped over greater distances. If the nation begins equipping new houses with solar-energy converters or heat-transfer devices to help relieve the fuel shortage, the number of man-hours necessary per unit will increase, both on and off the site.

It is therefore distinctly possible that housing's labor needs will eventually grow to the point where they severely tax the available pool of workers. At the same time, there is no reason to believe that the expectation of steadier employment will encourage building tradesmen to moderate their demands for higher wages. The combined effect of these two pressures may well be to push construction costs through the roof.

Beyond the basic shelter itself, the utility and social packages require labor. The size of their demand obviously depends on whether the new housing is located in areas that already have a network of services or on vacant land where everything must be developed from scratch.

But the possibility of using existing infrastructures depends in turn on the receptiveness of the affected neighborhoods to an influx of new residents. Thus the willingness of urban residents to live in close proximity with different social, economic, and racial groups—still a cause of sometimes bitter turmoil in modern America—will have a significant impact on the labor cost of new housing for the deprived. Just as the same question limited the availability of the nation's land resources by foreclosing some suburban land from use by the underhoused, so our urban social schisms threaten to increase the cost of helping this group within city limits.

The problems of location also impinge upon an even

more vital issue: the possibility of expanding the construction work force to include nonwhites in the ranks of the best-paid, most highly skilled building trades until they are represented in reasonable proportion to their share of the total population. This, at least, is how the problem might be formulated in the more progressive cities of the nation; elsewhere, discrimination against nonwhites is more primitive and blatant.

The breaking down of racial barriers is so rudimentary a bit of common justice that one hardly needs to expatiate on the matter. But it is equally important to remember that the unions came into existence and remain powerful because they prevent the price of human labor from sinking to the point at which it would have always remained if working people had not been permitted to bargain collectively. And if it is difficult to overcome the combination of fear and prejudice that tends to maintain local union exclusivity even when construction is booming, the task becomes virtually impossible when employment is irregular, for then the cardinal principle of all labor organization—that seniority, not outside favoritism, confers privileges—becomes not an abstract principle but the difference between working and not working.

The whole question of union discrimination is far too complex for this discussion of housing, but two points must be made. The first is the obvious one that progress in racial integration of the work force can be aided by government investment programmed to maintain a steady level of construction activity, making employment more dependable in an industry prone to cyclical ups and downs.

Second, attacks against union exclusivity become especially bitter when construction is undertaken in an area of high endemic unemployment among minority group members who are conscious of having been victimized by discriminatory practices generally. What is at issue in such cases is often not so much the ethnic composition of the union—it may even have a fair number of minority workers on the site—as the right of local residents to jobs on the projects. This movement proclaims that the neighborhood belongs properly to the people who live in it, and considers that an organization preferring the alleged rights of outsiders is "irrelevant" to the needs of those who are deprived in both income and housing.

The long-standing principle of trade unions in America—that they should organize around economic issues—has done more than any other single social institution to improve the position of countless formerly deprived Americans. No one who remembers this can view without a measure of alarm the "geographic" challenge to trade unionism. But it must also be recognized that here we are hearing, in a new accent, the very emphasis on localism that has made the construction unions at once highly decentralized and extremely powerful in the areas where they have won what amounts to a closed shop.

Unless the level of unemployment drops, the issue will become more acute and contractors will find it even more difficult to work out acceptable compromises between the unions and the local people who control the streets. Already some individuals have allegedly threatened to incite serious mob interference if they were not hired as "peacemakers." If the situation gets worse, contractors may well refuse to build in troublesome urban areas. Since the problem is not really amenable to solution on the national level, a modus vivendi in each locality will depend on painstaking negotiation between interested parties. Whatever the result, the spirit of localism will probably reduce the availability of trained labor to some extent, raising again the cost of housing for the urban poor.

All too often in the course of discussing housing labor, one forgets the requirements of the social package. In part, this embraces the relationships between those who live in multifamily housing and those who are responsible for its management.

In response to a manifest need for sound management, the federal government has established a National Center for Housing Management. Courses are now being given in this subject at a number of community colleges and similar institutions, just as courses in house planning, architecture, and economics are given at institutions of higher learning.

On the practical level, private foundations, often with government assistance, have set up model institutes and management firms to give professionalized training in everything from running a large housing cooperative to repairing small-apartment heating and plumbing systems. In addition, almost every major city has organizations of young people who are determined to make a personal impact on housing conditions. Some of them are showing low-income tenants how to improve housing conditions or manage buildings abandoned by their owners.

The most important manpower need, however, is to develop people with a so far undiscovered skill in remotivating and retraining for successful community life those multiproblem families who have demonstrated an incapacity to coexist peacefully with their neighbors. If, as some housing authorities believe, this group is beyond the reach of the behavioral sciences at the present time, a part of each major city will, as noted earlier, inevitably remain a slum. On the other hand, if this significant fraction of the badly housed can be brought to observe the minimal norms of conduct acceptable to the working poor, top priority should be given to this herculean task.

Early supporters of the housing reform movement sometimes promised the body politic that decent homes, sunlight, warmth in the winter, and adequate ventilation in summer would solve the social ills of all who lived in the slums. Although that faith seems naïve today, its appearance on the social scene was not fortuitous. One cannot justify investing in better housing for the poor if a small minority of them will destroy it for their neighbors. The national inability to deal with this problem is responsible for abandoned or decayed public housing projects in many cities and for a general disdain for public housing as a whole. Until this reality is widely understood, and a force of people is prepared to deal with it, no one can say that the human side of the housing resources picture equals the challenge.

ECONOMIC DEVELOPMENT

We customarily refer to our distant ancestors as cavemen because they lived in caves; we do not often reflect on the fact that they remained in caves until sufficient food could be provided to free some people from hunting long enough to build more congenial forms of habitation. In the modern context, the national economy must be sufficiently well developed to supply food, clothing, and recreational facilities, as well as shelter, for those employed in the construction and maintenance of housing.

Yet many citizens who impatiently demand that more resources be allocated to alleviate existing inequalities in American housing are unprepared to explain where the money should come from. The suggestions usually offered include the space program (not heard so often any more), the destructive highway trust fund (also fading from the public ear—the road network is nearly complete), the military budget (very often heard), or higher taxes (seldom heard from those who are expected to pay them). Unfortunately, cutting down on the resources being used in any sector of the economy reduces the nation's total usable wealth unless they are immediately set to work somewhere else.

In the case of housing, governmental decisions to appropriate new resources do not become effective instantly. In 1968–69, for example, Washington sought to stimulate employment and the gross national product by emphasizing housing production through monetary expansion and subsidies to private entrepreneurs. The desired housing boom did not come until 1971–72, because large-scale construction could not begin until local political contenders had been assuaged and until the normal restraints of capital markets had been circumvented.

Because of the time lag involved, any substantial shift of

resources to housing imperils economic activity in the present with relatively little assurance that it will be successfully stimulated by increased construction at a later date. In other words, new outlays for the benefit of the housing-deprived might have the result of diminishing the monetary wealth available for financing low-income housing. This paradox— that, under certain economic conditions, more resources may mean less wealth—derives from the function of money in the assertion of demand. If funds for housing were taken from the military budget, say, employment in the supporting defense industries would drop, lowering market demand for all consumer goods, including housing. The corresponding drop in tax revenues would then discourage local governments from accepting expensive obligations in a large-scale housing effort.

Of course, at a time when the total productive forces of the economy are operating at far less than full capacity, a different outcome might be hoped for. In these circumstances, a diversion of resources to housing, stimulated by government rewards and subsidies, could take up the slack in the economy, as seemed to happen between 1968–69 and 1971–72.

If a housing push for the poor, with all of the necessary changes in the utility and social packages, were piled on top of an already excessive demand for credit, the new construction would be not only extremely expensive but dangerous to the capital investment needed to meet other goals. A constant stream of goods and services of all kinds is necessary in a modern economy, particularly when it seeks to maintain or raise living standards for a growing population.

It is easy for breast-beaters to suggest that the United States is dedicated to maintaining too high a living standard for its people and that the rest of the world would benefit from lower consumption standards here. But in the short run the world suffers whenever America does not keep up its living standards, because it then buys fewer goods from foreign nations. The long run, which, if reached miraculously and instantaneously, might justify the claim that Americans should live less affluently, does not seem within the reach of a society whose affairs are governed by an electoral system exercised with the freedom of speech which Americans cherish.

It is easy to argue, too, that a system of government in the United States not wedded so firmly to the marketplace for the determination of human desires, or to the capital markets for the establishment of interest rates, might proceed differently. It is hard to prove this by consulting the facts. The nation that has achieved the greatest recent gains in housing, as measured by units constructed per capita, is Singapore, but conditions there are so different from America's that no meaningful comparison is possible. In the Soviet Union capital investment in industrial development and military preparation has taken priority over housing, although the level of crowding remains outrageously high by American standards. Under the government-administered price system based on a government-owned industrial plant, rents are cheap, but consumer goods like shoes and automobiles are not; there is a connection between the two facts.

The northern European countries most noted for their housing accomplishments have enjoyed, in the main, relatively stable population levels and export surpluses based on skilled labor that is partly remunerated by government welfare programs. In effect, such a combination nationalizes the production costs of exportable goods. The essentially homogeneous populations of Scandinavia are not afflicted with the racial strife and ethnic rivalries that complicate American housing policy. Yet despite a long history of cooperative ownership, these nations (especially Sweden) now seem to be encountering rising popular impatience with insistent government participation in the production of multifamily apartment buildings when there is a shortage of the one-family homes desired by a growing number of citizens.

At public meetings, after it has been shown that no panacea for our housing problems is to be found in imitating any foreign programs, someone always asks why interest has to be paid on mortgages. When the government needs battleships, this argument goes, it simply builds them, taxing people for the total cost instead of taking on a tremendous added expense in the form of accumulated interest charges. Why not do the same for low-income housing?

The truth of the matter is that much of the national debt was incurred in order to build battleships and fight wars; it was politically impossible to raise taxes enough to cover these expenditures even when victorious wars were widely regarded as essential to the nation's survival. Housing for the poor has never attained such unanimous support; meeting its capital costs by taxation alone would be politically unacceptable. No matter how progressive the tax law, such a program would impose a heavy burden even on many of the lower-income families we are trying to help.

Moreover, interest is not an artificial construct of a particular form of economic organization but an expression of the opportunity cost of capital—the cost of using goods and services for the production of one kind of long-term wealth rather than another. To put it another way, interest is a method of encouraging savings—a reward for a voluntary limitation of personal consumption that permits the marshaling of resources for capital projects such as housing. Although interest is not a perfect measure of social utility, it provides a means for choosing between alternative uses of resources.

The basic strategy of government housing programs has depended on minimizing the cost of capital. We must therefore understand how the money market functions and what constraints operate to shape the amount of capital available for housing purposes.

3

THE
MONEY MARKET

Drilling for oil is a high-risk enterprise because those holes in the ground are of little value if they fail to hit their target. Aside from a few bizarre creations of home owners with eccentric imaginations who act as their own architects and some creations by equally eccentric architects acting as their own clients, most dwellings acceptable to any one family will usually be suitable for at least some others. This universal acceptability, and the fact that houses are reasonably secure from being dragged away or misappropriated, assure that the provision of housing is generally less speculative than digging oil wells.

Since the risks of oil wildcatting make it an inappropriate investment for widows, orphans, and savings banks, it must be financed by wealthy speculators with other substantial assets. But permanent housing debt, secured largely by the putative market value of the structure itself, has been regarded for many years as a proper investment for the institutions that manage the funds of widows, orphans, and other citizens who have to be satisfied with lower rewards in return for greater safety.

The expectation (often in the form of a written commitment) that an investing institution will put up long-term mortgage money for housing makes possible the extension of short-term building loans. These building loans, coupled with a relatively small entrepreneurial commitment (in some government-assisted programs, no risk capital is involved at all), finance the actual construction. While the initial borrowing is of relatively short duration, the interest on it nevertheless contributes significantly to the development cost of the building.

The interest rate on the permanent financing is, of course, a larger factor in the ultimate cost of housing. Nearly as important are the terms of repayment, or "amortization," of the mortgage debt and its ratio to the development cost. In the case of owner-occupied single-family housing (which under FHA regulations may have as many as four families in residence), a high ratio of loan to value or cost reduces the size of the down payment required of the owner and thereby enlarges the number of eligible buyers. As a rule, too, stretching out the terms of a mortgage lowers the monthly repayments, though it adds to the total amount of interest paid.

For the consumer, the mortgage interest rate is by far the major item in housing cost: On a $30,000 unit, the difference between a mortgage at 7.5 percent and one at 9.5 percent works out to approximately $50 a month, whether rental or owner-occupied. That implies a very different clientele for the finished housing, which affects the potential mortgageability of the house, which affects the availability of construction money, which affects the overall mobilization of resources for housing.

Consequently, a nation that wants to achieve growth in housing has to create an atmosphere favorable to mortgages by encouraging low interest rates, high debt ratios, and long-term repayment. Most Western countries have found themselves involved in precisely this process, even at times when housing policy needs—low interest rates, for instance—interfere with other economic goals, like controlling inflation.

In the United States, however, despite concerted efforts at all levels of government, the trend of general interest rates over the past twenty-five years has been almost unrelentingly upward. In fairness, though, the government has succeeded in keeping mortgage interest rates lower than they would otherwise be. To understand how this has been accomplished, it is first necessary to review the major sources of housing mortgage money and the various economic forces that influence the level of interest rates.

The vast majority of permanent residential mortgages in America are made by institutions of four types: commercial banks, savings and loan associations, life insurance companies, and (in eighteen states) mutual savings banks. All of these institutions accept money from the public and invest it in interest-bearing obligations. To attract deposits, they may offer interest income, long-term benefits (like life insurance), or services such as checking accounts. Their customers have the right to withdraw their money at will, though sometimes subject to the payment of a penalty charge.

As makers of mortgage loans, they all benefit from forms of treatment and powers under the law that differ from those extended to other types of financial institutions. Mutual savings banks, life insurance companies, and savings and loan associations are regarded as trustees of their depositors' money, so that only a portion of their actual earnings are considered to be income for tax purposes. The commercial banks are treated for the most part like other corporations under the income tax law, but they enjoy the enviable power of creating money on which they charge interest: When a customer takes out a loan, the amount lent is customarily credited to his account, thus increasing the bank's total deposits—on paper—and giving it more money with which to make more loans. In practice, federal and state laws reinforce the bank's natural disinclination to lend money to borrowers of dubious credit.

When the demand for loans becomes very heavy and interest rates rise, commercial banks usually find that the balances in their customers' non-interest-bearing checking accounts are down, forcing the banks themselves to borrow—and pay interest on—funds to support their existing and new loans within the federally prescribed reserve limits.

Under the same circumstances, depositors in the other types of savings and mortgage institutions also become restive, withdrawing money to buy bonds and other obligations that pay higher interest rates. This process, which has been given the elaborate name of "disintermediation," forces the mortgage institutions to pay higher interest rates on their depositors' savings or, in the case of life insurance companies, to seek higher-yielding investments so that they can pay larger dividends on their policies.

Keeping interest rates low for residential mortgages involves separate kinds of activities that sometimes conflict with each other. On the one hand, the institutions that customarily extend mortgages require some sort of insulation from the rest of the money market, so their depositors will not be successfully tempted to disintermediate. Obviously, a large money supply helps. This is a favorite theme of American populism, given its most vivid expression by William Jennings Bryan's "You shall not crucify mankind upon a cross of gold."

It is inevitable that some money should leak from institutions which are regulated as to interest rates and that it should flow into other forms of investment that are free from such control. A few states compel mutual savings banks to invest a certain percentage of their assets within the state, in the expectation that this will keep mortgage money at home and thus produce lower mortgage rates. Yet such laws can do nothing to prevent the depositors in the state from withdrawing their money and putting it in less regulated investments or out-of-state banks that pay higher interest rates. In short, state or federal attempts to clamp a lid on mortgage interest rates at times of high credit demand serve mainly to reduce the supply of mortgage money, which pushes interest rates up in any case. Thus the populist policy wrongly timed may well lead to an antipopulist eventuality.

The special income tax treatment accorded the principal mortgage institutions has some effect in keeping down the interest rates they would otherwise have to charge their customers. But this is merely the simplest form of government activity on behalf of moderate mortgage rates. While mortgage interest rates have been rising, the tax liabilities of some institutions (notably the life insurance companies) have increased; and so has the rigor of federal efforts to make savings bank depositors report their interest earnings and pay income taxes on them. Here, too, the populist motive of forcing the banking institutions to pay their "fair share" of the national tax burden has contributed in some measure to the antipopulist objective of keeping interest rates high.

The first major government move to bring about moderate interest rates was the establishment of the Federal Housing Administration in 1934. Originally a Depression measure, the FHA subsequently became a long-term enterprise. Intended as a government corporation to insure mortgage lenders against less in return for premiums paid, the FHA operated over the years at a profit: The combination of its premium income, the interest earned on the investment of that income, and the proceeds of sales of the residential properties it acquired when insured mortgages went into default, has substantially exceeded its payments to banks to make good their losses. This profitability drew private competitors into the field. A present the FHA portfolio is primarily made up of high-risk mortgages which are avoided by private insurers (who charge lower premiums and cover only a part of the risk). In 1976 FHA insurance of multifamily housing became a vital part of the process of constructing low-rent developments.

Besides protecting qualified mortgage lenders and influencing the quality of construction through what it calls its "property standards," the FHA stipulates a maximum rate of interest that it will permit on an insured mortgage. Since interest represents a compensation for calculated risk as well as for the use of money, the safety offered by FHA insurance probably had a moderating effect on mortgage rates up to the end of World War II. As the demand for mortgage loans grew in the housing boom that followed World War II, interest rates generally moved higher than the maximum permitted under FHA ceilings.

Accordingly, a discounting practice developed, under which the lending institutions advance less money than the face value of the mortgage, but the borrower ultimately pays back the full face amount. The difference equalizes the gap between the FHA maximum and the going market rate of interest. While the practice may seem somehow abhorrent, the FHA recognizes that the supply of mortgage money would otherwise shrink, and tolerates it; at the same time, the official FHA rate has soared from 4.5 to 8.5 percent to attract a flow of money into mortgages.

A second major government effort to minimize mortgage rates involves the curious case of public housing. As this program emerged in the late 1930s, local housing authorities were encouraged to enter into Annual Contributions Contracts with the federal government. These contracts guaranteed that the federal government would itself repay moneys the localities borrowed to cover the development costs of projects to house families of low income. In addition, interest paid by local housing authorities on their borrowings from private bond buyers was exempt from federal and (within the state involved) state income taxes.

Investors are always willing to purchase tax-exempt obligations that pay a lower rate of interest than they would insist upon receiving if the receipts were taxable. This process saves little or no money for the federal government in the long run, because the loss in income tax revenues may well exceed the saving that the federal government makes in the annual contributions to the local housing authorities whose obligations are federally tax-exempt. But the loss in taxes is less visible than the amount of the subsidy. The latter requires affirmative federal action; the former is noticed only by close students of government finance. The notion, therefore, of using federal income tax exemption on the interest received by the owners of local bonds has spread widely through the field of residential mortgage investment.

New York was the first state to take full advantage of the device. In 1955 its Limited Profit Housing Company Law authorized the sale of state bonds to raise mortgage money for private housing whose occupants would be persons of limited income and whose owners would be restricted to a 6 percent annual net return on their equity investment. The city of New York was given similar powers. Since then approximately $3 billion in mortgage money has been put into so-called middle-income housing developments in the state; the debt-service saving resulting from the tax exemption of bond interest, averaging about 2 percent per annum, amounts to roughly about $60 million per year. The idea proved to be contagious, and some thirty states now have established finance agencies to sell tax-exempt bonds for housing mortgages.

As might be expected, the tax exemption has had its opponents in Washington. The Nixon administration at one point suggested that the Internal Revenue Code be amended to discourage use of the privilege for local bonds floated for housing mortgage purposes unconnected with the central activities of local government. Many fiscal experts have recommended that tax-exempt municipal bonds for any purpose be terminated, and that part of the increase be made up by the federal government through direct subsidization. Congress remains divided on the issue. Such a permissive provision turned up in the Housing and Community Development Act of 1974, but it has not been put into effect.

Meanwhile, the tax-exempt device is no longer working as well as it used to. In the first place, the total construction and operating cost of multifamily urban housing has risen so high that even a 2 percent reduction in the mortgage rate leaves these buildings beyond the reach of a much broader spectrum of families than in the past. Monthly rents in new developments financed by New York's Limited Profit Housing Company now reach $100 per room, as against $21 per room fifteen years ago. Family incomes have increased by a much smaller percentage.

Secondly, the growth in local and state debt has been tremendous over the last two decades, although state governments have generally been able to increase their own tax rates sufficiently to keep themselves fiscally on a sound basis. The growth of local government debt will ultimately increase the supply of tax-exempt bonds until so many will be available that high interest rates will be needed to attract buyers. The time will come—if the growth continues—when local government obligations will be unsalable. The time came for New York State in 1974 and early 1975. It came with such a vengeance that the usefulness of local borrowing for housing mortgage purposes may turn out to have been permanently destroyed unless the federal government decides to exercise the unused provisions of the 1974 Act and insures buyers of state housing obligations by guaranteeing or co-insuring them.

The federal government seems disinclined to insure these local government loans for the very good reason that it would have little or no way to protect itself against imprudence. It would be obliged to pay all the losses incurred by bond buyers whenever a project with an insured local mortgage proved itself unable to meet its debt service. Besides not protecting the federal government against what might be called the "normal" risks of local housing finance agency operations, the mere *fact* of the guarantee would probably increase the readiness of local housing agencies to undertake new risks with the money advanced by their bond buyers.

It is not so easy for the federal government to devise a workable method to cut down the risk of local government mortgage lending. Public opinion exerts its pressures on federal policy makers. Even if public opinion were always in

favor of insuring only fiscally sound loans, a gross improba-
bility, the technical problems of evaluating the soundness of
socially desirable loans baffled the FHA in the course of the
1972–73 housing boom, and has become no easier since.

This problem pushes the federal official in the direction
of the so-called Co-Insurance option under the 1974 Act. Co-
Insurance offers the federal government's protection against a
major part, but not all, of the risk in making mortgage loans
for housing purposes. The idea is that if a lending institution
recognizes that it has something at risk, it will use far more
discretion in approving a loan than it might if its entire investment were protected by mortgage insurance. The Department of Housing and Urban Development has concluded that
self-interest will be a more effective guardian of the public investment than any handbook of safe mortgage practices which
might be devised by the FHA or any other responsible government agency.

Further complicating the raising of money for housing
purposes is the reluctance of even those institutions which
traditionally use residential mortgage investment as a major
part of their fiscal policy to continue to feel the same way
about mortgages in the current financial climate. Unprecedented fluctuations in interest rates, wide swings of deposit
inflows and outflows, unstable operating costs in the apartment house field, and neighborhood changes that occur with
dramatic speed and that may have devastating effects upon
the value of residential real estate—all of these have continued
to discourage financial institutions from making commitments
in apartment houses in urban areas. Even if one hopes that
future housing trends will move toward smaller types of
house, one must recognize that no institution is prepared to
make a large number of mortgage loans unless it is convinced
that it would always be able to sell them in a reasonably favorable market.

The 1974 Act relied on the state housing finance agencies
to provide the bulk of mortgage funds for the social sector. It
now appears that most mortgages written to take advantage of

the Act's subsidy provisions (the so-called Section 8 program) will have to be private mortgages, presumably insured by the FHA or co-insured by banks as well as the federal government. Even if the Section 8 subsidy program is rewritten by Congress to give private lenders the same long-term subsidy protection given to the state housing agencies under the present act, mortgages in volume will require not only the protection of guarantees or co-insurance, but also the perpetuation and expansion of a secondary mortgage market assisted by the government.

The federal government has in fact established such a secondary market; ultimately, this market will provide the long-term funds needed to sustain mortgages for the urban centers. These funds will come from the sale of obligations of the major secondary market institution—the Government National Mortgage Association (government-owned) and the Federal National Mortgage Association (privately owned). GNMA is empowered to borrow money from the Treasury and it uses these funds to absorb losses on the mortgages that have been sold to it, enabling it to resell these mortgages to FNMA at a lower price than it paid for them. The government absorbs the loss to encourage private purchase of FNMA's bonds, debentures, and notes.

Although the tax-exemption feature of local borrowing served to help *local* governments effectuate a middle-income housing program, Congress had to devise a less indirect method for reducing mortgage interest in 1963, when it decided to support *federal* middle-income housing under private ownership. Federal obligations are *not* tax-exempt. As a result, the 221(d)3 Program depended on an interest subsidy from the federal government. This law insured mortgages carrying a 3.5 percent interest rate. Occupancy was limited to persons whose income fell within certain narrow ranges and the ownership was in the hands of a corporation controlled as to dividends and profits. Of course, 3.5 percent was far below the market rate even in 1963, and no bank would make such a mortgage unless it could immediately dispose of it at face value—a procedure made possible through the Federal National Mortgage Association (FNMA). "Fanny Mae" was then a government corporation that bought up the mortgage at par and continued to accept the 3.5 percent interest from the mortgagor while absorbing much higher interest charges on the money it borrowed to pay the originating institutional mortgagee. Ultimately, FNMA made its mortgages directly.

This system did furnish relatively low-cost mortgages for special groups in the population. Its problems were partly fiscal, partly connected with ownership, and partly the result of insufficient attention to the social package of services. Fiscally, the subsidy was too small to help very much. The ownership of 221(d)3 projects was sometimes shrewd without being enlightened; sometimes enlightened without being shrewd—poor management followed. The 221(d)3 program did not include provisions for social services for residents, although many could not solve their problems by themselves.

The program was finally stopped, in the course of a typical federal policy zigzag, because the holding of a mortgage that produced less interest than the government itself paid to borrow the money was construed by the Office of Management and Budget to be a burden on the national debt limit. As a result, Fanny Mae was divided into the private and public functions: a new Government National Mortgage Association (GNMA) in effect provided the subsidies needed to enable FNMA to carry the mortgages as a private institution. By this bureaucratic surgery, the total charge to the national debt was reduced to the annual interest deficit instead of the very much larger face amount of the mortgages involved.

As housing costs rose still higher, Congress adopted a new interest subsidization plan, also limited to people with incomes too large for public projects but too small for the open market—FHA 235 for single-family housing and FHA 236 for multifamily housing. Under these programs the government would pay to the mortgage lender each year the difference between the debt service needed to carry a near-market-rate mortgage (equal to 6 percent at first, but raised ultimately to 8.5 percent interest plus amortization) and a mortgage with 1 percent interest plus amortization. This interest subsidy reduced the amount of rent necessary to cover the actual mortgage payments. FHA 236 was abandoned by Congress at the prodding of the Nixon and Ford administrations. The objections stemmed from the continued rise of housing operating costs and the allegedly high cost of FHA 236 to the government. FHA 236 was, indeed, an expensive program, combining an interest subsidy with special tax deductions for the owners. But it is not more expensive than public housing or the government leasing of units in buildings financed by private sources (Section 23).

Ironically, the Housing and Community Development Act of 1974 more or less forced on the Ford administration a more expensive subsidy program than FHA 235 and 236 had been. It could also be described as a more realistic subsidy program than either of these, or perhaps it could be called the post-oil-embargo housing subsidy. Although the Administration did not say so, the interest subsidy programs like 221(d)3 and 236 failed to provide for increases in the costs of operating the buildings built to take advantage of the periodic subsidies. The rents established in these buildings reflected a greatly reduced capital charge (because of the mortgage interest subsidy) but the actual predicted operating costs—fuel, electricity, labor, real property taxes, etc.—were left to be paid by the residents, irrespective of whether their incomes rose as fast. Families became eligible if their income did not exceed a stipulated maximum, and they were required to pay at least 25 percent of their income as rent.

For many of these families, the payment of rent equal to 25 percent of a modest income (some paid even more because their incomes were far below the maximum limit) involved severe hardship. As operating costs rose, particularly in the wake of higher oil prices, the rents had to be drastically increased because the operating costs originally consumed an unexpectedly large part of the rent dollar. The result was undeniable hardship, followed by rent delinquencies, followed by move-outs and insufficient maintenance, followed by mortgage delinquencies, and FHA repossessions. Clearly, these dire events did not take place in every 236 project. Many, particularly those located in areas attractive to families whose incomes approached the maximum, have remained fiscally sound. But in the 1970s Congress and the Administration agreed (it was one of the rare cases of agreement between the Democratic Congress and the Republican Administration) that federal subsidy aid should help low-income families. Accordingly, the Section 8 provision of the 1974 Housing and Community Development Act greatly increases the amount of money available per family for housing subsidies, and lowers somewhat the income limits for eligibility (at least it *requires* that a stipulated percentage of very low-income families be admitted to each new project in which all units are to receive Section 8 subsidies). The new law does not permit the use of "exception limits" for families with incomes above the maximum for initial occupancy. To balance this with economic reality, the law now allows the government to establish a maximum reserve subsidy, equal to the whole rent of a new unit—thus a family with zero income would find its entire rent paid. Since not even the families on welfare have zero income, the reserve is considerably more than will be needed on initial occupancy, and will be available to cover increased operating costs so that the families' own contribution to rent will never exceed 25 percent of their own income.

4

THE PROBLEM
OF PURPOSE

The patience-straining difficulties of dealing with ma-
moth bureaucracies have turned many a youthful socialist
into an enthusiastic fan of the free market; housing has provided a significant stimulus in this direction to many, for it is
the commodity in which government, in the United States,
has most deeply involved itself. It may also be the commodity
causing the greatest dissatisfaction. For many years, government interest in housing was simple, designed to protect people and property from injury and destruction from fire. Standards for chimney and fireplace construction and restrictions
against flammable roofs were the first fruit of that government interest.

The assertion of even so primitive a government interest
in the quality of a commodity brings in the course of time
two inevitable consequences. The first is an expansion of the
early interest into associated fields. The second is the ultimate
requirement of subsidies. Expansion of government interest
follows logically because if safety against fire is promoted by

prescribing chimney and roof construction, good men and women are certain to persuade their fellow citizens that walls and floors are equally deserving of attention; that quick access to water helps to confine a blaze; and that therefore reservoirs, pipes, fire hydrants, and standpipe systems and sprinklers in bigger buildings are an essential part of fire protection. Nor does the response to the purpose of fire protection stop with these concerns. Serious protection against fire involves such seemingly unrelated items of architectural design as the width of corridors, the spacing of doors, the arrangement of apartments within a multiple dwelling so that no occupant in the building will be at any time more than a stipulated distance from a safe exit. Naturally, the characteristics of a safe means of egress must be carefully defined.

Ultimately—and one may be sure that the end is not in sight, for new materials and new styles of construction design continually appear and require evaluation from the point of view of fire protection—the elementary caution against fire has determined a very large part of the appearance, size, design, and, supremely, the cost of structures. At all times the greater the density of population, the more complicated the process of fire protection, because the greater the risk of contagion. Thus, one inescapable consequence of accepting the governmental role in defending citizenry against fire is to increase the cost of construction by so serious a factor that a free market for the ultimate product is no longer truly reliable. A free market supposes that the interrelationships between people remain so tenuous, and the social and physical distances between them remain so reassuring, that the public need not concern itself with standards so expensive that they distort the price of the commodity. If a consumer lives by himself in the desert, no one cares if he should choose to spend his money lighting matches rather than listening to Beethoven. But if he lives in a city, its government must concern itself with the safety of his pastimes. Even if our match lighter is a totally objectionable firebug whose presence in the "community" is clearly dispensable, and whose demise might even stimulate local rejoicing, citizens will not allow him to burn himself to death, screaming, on the fifth floor of a walkup tenement without making some effort to save him. His death endangers the neighbors. The incremental cost of the fire escape is imposed on his budget, willy-nilly, in order to provide a measure of safety for the fireman who must risk his life to calm the community conscience and allay its fears of contagion.

Therefore, it follows that the government, having imposed minimum standards for fire protection on all who build in a settled area, has also made a totally free market impossible, by increasing the cost of construction without regard to whether those who must in the end pay for it are willing or prepared to do so. Nor will it answer to say that the government should keep its bureaucratic tendencies firmly in hand and refuse to take even a first step to prevent fires or reduce their spread. This is not to say that the free-marketer may not argue that in the end perceptive customers will watch their neighbors burning to death, and draw from this the inference that when they build their own houses they must protect themselves against a similarly melancholy fate. The argument, however, is naïve.

For a free market in other matters will, with respect to housing, inevitably bring with it a method of establishing general standards about fire protection. Someone, for example, will stumble upon the notion of pooling fire risk through insurance. Experience will reveal that losses of the insurer are minimized when buildings are constructed to stipulated standards. Once again, we will find that in order to buy insurance the owner of a building will have to design it in conformity with a purely private code of fire safety which will be as binding upon basic housing costs as the public codes have already proved to be. Even in the absence of legal codes, mortgage lenders will sooner or later—and probably sooner—announce that they will offer loans only to those whose buildings are insured against fire. This private insistence will be as effective as law.

Accept the faintest degree of public interest in the matter of fire, and you will find, as a result, that there is no stopping place for public policy short of forcing a major change in the cost of housing. The public interest itself has created a major impediment to that swirling mix of demand and production, the free market.

The cost added by such basics as fire protection brings along with it the second consequence; one can only justify the increased cost by a new definition of the ultimate objective of public policy. The willingness to increase the cost of housing for fire protection cannot be cut short when one has assured oneself as to fire safety. The housing product has become more expensive; therefore, it must be protected against other risks. And each time the cost of housing rises, society assumes the responsibility of meeting those costs which the residents can't pay. Thus, while the earliest housing legislation deals with protecting the community from such clear and common dangers as fire, disease, and structural collapse, the arguments marshaled to support these changes in law and elevation of standards contain a large measure of social and philosophical objectives to improve the lives of the residents. And society must be prepared to pay for so important an achievement.

Combing the reports of the endless investigative committees on housing conditions in the large cities—London, New York, and Boston—the reader finds an inseparable intertwining of the apparent initial criteria of housing improvement and the secondary societal aims. All of the investigative committees in the nineteenth century share the horror of their members over the paucity of light and fresh air that the poorly housed have access to. They discuss the relationship between disease, particularly tuberculosis, and the physical matrix of family life. But gradually, as they record the impact of tuberculosis on family structure, the concern shifts from the fear of contagion itself to a stress on the relationship between freedom from disease and a good family life. This shift led to a discussion of the relationship between good housing and a good family life. Although the progression may well have been imperceptible to the propagandists who articulated it, the promise of housing reform gradually came to include the promise that good housing would improve the social conditions of life and help the miserable families of the slums to breathe freely. "Let in the sun," said Mayor La Guardia of New York in urging housing reform in the 1930s, and it is impossible to read these words without recognizing that he was referring not only to the advantages of sunlight in stimulating the body's production of certain vitamins. The opening of the dark recesses of the human spirit to the regenerating qualities of light and the consequent spiritual renascence were equally on his mind.

Yet even as the contemporary reader reflects on the apparent and somewhat charming naïveté that associated light with societal improvement, a certain misgiving arises over the reliability of the implied promise. People have been moved from darkness into light, but the societal benefits remain unequally distributed. Some families have benefited remarkably from access for the first time to generally accepted standards of room occupancy, room size, and fresh air. Their children's performances in school have improved, and the whole community has been improved by their change in fortune. But other families or households have not reacted similarly. Indeed, for some the darkness serves to shield the community at large from having to notice how dramatically the conduct of some of the poor deviates from generally accepted community standards. The result of the exposure has been in part a revulsion against the disappointment and against the housing movement which made the exposure take place. This sentiment has also been accompanied by another response, perhaps not heard so frequently in the very recent past: the claim that it is an inhumane mistake to place disorderly households in a physical matrix in which they will be expected to impose restriction on their conduct in the interests of good-neighborliness. "You are," the riposte to the housing reformers insisted, "trying to impose middle-class standards on the poor."

The desirability of family life has been challenged by some, but the conflict stirred by other social policy objectives on housing is much more heated. Sometimes the objectives themselves interfere with the marshaling of economic forces which are needed to make construction or rehabilitation possible. Finally, these social objectives and the special policy which collectively they comprise have rarely been examined in any systematic way by those responsible for adding them to housing law and regulation. As a result, a complicated body of sanctions and requirements has been built into the governmental connection with housing until, like the work rules of a railroad, they impose a burden which, taken seriously, would stop everything, good and bad.

One might divide the social policy issues in housing under three convenient headings, recognizing that there are inevitable matters for decision in which the issues tend to overlap. The first such heading might be the determination of eligibility for governmental assistance in housing. The second heading involves the question of tenure: what are the terms on which those found eligible for governmental assistance are to continue to live in the premises they occupy; what are their rights as against the owner, public or merely publicly assisted? Finally come the thorny questions involving the nature of the community, or, if one prefers it, the "settlement" of which the assisted housing is to be a part. Housing, as a by-product of its almost inescapable longevity, determines the mode of a human settlement for many years, far longer surely than even the most prescient forecaster can see into the future. It is possible, therefore, that substantial funds might be committed to the construction of housing precisely where it will not be needed; or that the housing population will have been selected or the specific sites chosen in a way which perpetuates social arrangements that will be unacceptable over the years.

With respect to the first of the social policy issues—who shall live in public housing?—the question to be resolved is whether there is to be a means test for those who benefit from public assistance in housing or whether publicly assisted housing should be available to anyone who wants to live in it, irrespective of income. Lest this seem too simple a question, and the answer—"of course, assistance should be provided only to those who need it"—too obvious, it must be noted that while the United States has characteristically opted for restricting housing assistance to those who need it, Britain has tended to proceed in the opposite direction, priding itself for many years on its veneration of the right of privacy. As we noted earlier, American practice does in fact provide some major housing subsidies without examination of the economic need of the recipient, including among these subsidies the tax deductibility of mortgage interest and real property taxes. There are no limits on the deductibility of these taxes; in effect, the owner of the most highly valued home in the town may get the benefit of the largest federal tax deduction. Another subsidy without means test in either Britain or America is the local subsidy, paid for indirectly by the municipality but immediately by the owners of rent-controlled premises, which rent control offers to tenants. Every day brings proposals to the local administrators of rent control suggesting that the level of rents be adjusted to the level of the tenants' incomes. This proposal is rarely adopted in a simple form because of the great volume of paperwork it would involve; there is no way in which the income of each household can be checked without violating the confidentiality of income tax returns, or establishing a municipal income verification bureau that would resemble the bureaucracy of the Internal Revenue Service itself.

In the case of direct federal subsidies to make housing available at the requisite quality level to those who cannot otherwise afford it, present federal law—in the case of Section 8 of the Housing and Community Development Act of 1974—limits housing subsidies to those whose earnings fall below the median income level of the market area. This sounds more precise than it is, because arguments can readily develop over what constitutes a "market area." If the market area is taken to be the inner city, any inner city, its median income level will be lower than if the market area is taken to include the suburbs. If the suburbs are included in the Department of Housing and Urban Development definition of a market area, the median income will be higher than if the suburbs are excluded, and the subsidies will therefore be paid to families earning more income.

While it seems logical to offer subsidies only to those families whose income is below the middle for the area in which they live, the Section 8 provision mandates an abrupt cutoff of subsidy at a specific income limit. This produces curious anomalies. Thus, if the income limit for assistance in a specific market area is $12,000 for a family of four, the family whose income is only a few dollars below that figure can live in a new apartment house qualifying for Section 8, and pay less than $3,000 per year (one quarter of its income) as rent. The federal government will pay the difference between one quarter of their income and the actual approved market rent for their apartment. Another family, living in the same building but earning slightly over the income limit, a few hundred dollars per year more than the first family, would receive no federal help at all. That family would be required to pay the market rent, which might be as high as $6,000 per year, or more (depending on HUD's definition of a fair rent in a newly constructed residential building in the area).

Even if the formulators of social policy agree, then, that government assistance should be reserved for those who need it economically, and even if they agree further to meet the proof of eligibility by accepting affidavits on income accompanied by government spot checks of actual tax returns in the presence of those seeking assistance, the selection of who would be helped involves practical and theoretical difficulties. Income limits should be designed to eliminate inequitable treatment of families whose levels of need are much less disparate than the amount of help they currently receive from the national government. But the political difficulties in supplying *overt* subsidies to those who are not in the bottom half of the income range of a local population cannot easily be overcome. This remains true even though all the legislators who vote on such a measure know perfectly well that covert subsidies are continuously being given without any means test at all.

The tradition of geographical mobility introduces another social policy issue in housing, because of the implicit conflict between the encouragement of personal mobility and the sustaining of neighborhoods. American constitutional policy has traditionally frowned on barriers to free migration from one part of the nation to another. The elimination of state sovereignty over its own population was one of the great achievements of the new nation. There is, therefore, no state residence requirement for an applicant for federal housing assistance. Nor is citizenship necessary, so long as the applicant is a legal resident.

The current federal Section 8 program which provides assistance to residents in existing housing units carries the opportunity for mobility to its limits. In the unmodified workings of the economic system, one's own limited purchasing power in turn limits and defines one's choice of a place to live. Whether we admit it or not, limited purchasing power has tended to strengthen neighborhood stability by making movement *from* a neighborhood expensive. With a Section 8 subsidy allocation, however, a neighborhood family may decide to move elsewhere, taking its housing subsidy with it, and leaving empty the unit in which it first received its subsidy. This hyper-mobility tends not only to ignore the economics of apartment house operation, and thus to discourage reinvestment and rehabilitation of tired, worn buildings. It also militates against the use of subsidies to strengthen neighborhoods, an aim which would be achieved by limiting the mobility of subsidy recipients in the same way that the limits of their purchasing power limits the ability of nonsubsidized people to move. A neat and clean resolution of conflicting objectives—mobility and stability—is not yet in sight.

Perhaps the most serious defect in American housing

which advocates of social policy have generally wished to correct has been racial segregation. So much has been written on this topic that the bare facts have often been obscured and forgotten. Segregation by race has been characteristic of American cities for many decades, enforced by the refusal of white families to rent or sell to nonwhites—Negroes, Orientals, and Latins with dark skins. Nor was this all. Patterns of exclusion by refusing to rent or sell to members of atypical religious, ethnic, and nationality groups were equally common. The patterns of exclusion were complicated to some extent by patterns of self-segregation, based on the wish of many members of the excluded groups to remain in contact with their fellows. Until 1964, it was the frank policy of the national government not to impose any social policy corrective to the patterns of exclusion and self-segregation of American residential settlement. Indeed, the federal government, through the FHA's mortgage insurance criteria, questioned the soundness of the economics of any development which avowedly pursued a policy of racial integration.

The revulsion against a system of exclusion peaked after the Supreme Court decision on public school segregation; Secretary Robert C. Weaver of HUD worked diligently to wipe out from the FHA underwriting practices the suspicion of unsoundness which had been associated with interracial developments. This was a difficult task. One cannot persuade appraisers to change their minds about a value system overnight, particularly when it is true that a number of the interracial developments were, in fact, economically unsound. This does not mean they were unsound because they were interracial. In many, probably most cases, the unsoundness, if it existed, reflected the undesirability of the site selected for the development; existing segregated patterns made the acquisition of better sites difficult.

It can be said with some justice that social policy has teetered since 1964 between two polar views of what the evil was that the school segregation decision had sought to correct. Clearly, if no consensus existed as to the nature of the evil, no consensus could be possible on the proper course of correction. One view was that the existence of segregated schools, segregated housing, and segregated communities was itself the evil. Those who adhered to this view concluded that the object of social policy should be the achievement of integration. While there was surely room for disagreement over which was the best means to obtain integration, the removal of legal barriers to integration was by itself insufficient.

The alternative view is that the evil which the Supreme Court sought to correct was the evil of exclusion on irrelevant criteria such as race—the use of public and private force to prevent people from living where they wished to live or to attend school, even if they had the economic means to do so. If this is the evil, then to correct it means to strike down all public and private attempts at exclusion, but to avoid interfering with the process of self-selection of a school or, more particularly, of a place to live (which usually imposes a geographical imperative on the process of selecting a school).

Clearly both positions have their weakness. In the pursuit of integration as a goal of governmental housing policy, adherents to the first position sometimes find themselves in the awkward position of refusing admission to any development of more than a stipulated number of black families. Believing, probably with justification, that the presence of a large number of black families in any development will discourage white families from entering it, these advocates have formulated a policy of exclusion which resembles the very policies that evoked moral outrage in the past. The excluded families are in fact denied access to housing as sternly as if the motive for their exclusion were malignant instead of benign. Somewhere down the road to the future, advocates of this social policy may find themselves accepting a significant limitation of the freedom with which Americans choose housing; if the imposition of black quotas fails to stimulate white applications, someone will be certain to advocate that whites be *assigned* to live where they will produce integration or, at the least, forfeit any possible further federal assistance.

Those who argue against government integration by affirmative action must admit, for their part, that the process of breaking down the segregation of blacks will be laboriously slow, and that much of black self-segregation results from the effects of generations of inferior status, so that, in a sense, it cannot be considered voluntary in the way in which the self-segregation of other ethnic groups, unidentifiable on the basis of skin color, *will* their self-segregation.

In any case, social policy on this issue poses serious problems for housing politics, and for economics. Advocates of black power, who include, in this sense, almost all black elected officials, have not complained unduly about the use of black quotas in integrated housing developments. It may be that some black leadership welcomes limits on the number of black families who will move from their present addresses to new, integrated housing. A policy that keeps blacks from moving in large numbers to integrated housing keeps them concentrated in neighborhoods in which they are the majority, and their present elected leaders can look forward to continuing in office. Certainly, blacks, like all other groups, should enjoy the choice of whether to live in heterogeneous or homogeneous neighborhoods; this tenet means that each family should have the choice, not that leaders should be able to choose for them. On the economic side, holding apartments for which there are applicants eligible in every way but race makes the tenanting of the housing a long-drawn-out and expensive procedure. The issue has not finally been resolved between integration and non-forced segregation as the basic aims of policy.

In the preamble to the National Housing Act, there is the statement that the objective of national policy is the provision of a home for "every American family." Undefined social policy swirls around the meaning of the word "family." For many years, local housing authorities exercised great restraint in renting to single persons; many had minimum age limits for their admission, evidencing a fear that the projects would be tarnished if they were used for what were formerly called "immoral purposes." Similarly, public housing managers have avoided couples unsanctified by marriage; while few absolute bans on unmarried couples were found, it was necessary for unmarried families to establish that they had a stable household, with a record of years of cohabitation, in order to qualify for admission.

These restrictions have faded in many parts of the country, as the general notion of what constitutes morally acceptable conduct has changed. Should homosexual couples be admitted to housing assisted by government subsidies? Should state government institute lawsuits to establish the right of newly released mental patients to rent a block of apartments in a federally subsidized privately owned housing development? Should "families" include single women who have had no husband but nevertheless have children (their own) living with them? In short, should federal housing subsidies take any notice whatever of the personal behavior of those who receive their benefit?

It is easy to answer these questions all very grandly with a ringing affirmation of the right to live as one wishes, free from interference by government agents acting as peeping Toms. It was similarly grand to criticize those official raiders who descended on public assistance households in search of evidence that the vanished husband (on whose absence public support depended) was, in fact, living under the bed. The public—even the respectably liberal public—is at this stage of the nation's history genuinely concerned about the legitimacy of claims for welfare assistance. It is possible that the future will bring increased demands for a set of behavior standards in which federal assistance to housing will again play a normative role.

From the point of view of social policy makers, housing is not simply a structure. The promise, noted earlier, that housing will have a beneficial effect on human life has not been forgotten. Housing officials, who codified for the national government, the states, and many of the cities such meticulous details as the size of rooms and the structural arrangements for housing eligible for subsidy, followed principles laid out in the late 1930s by the Committee on the Hygiene of Housing established by the American Public Health Association. Reading the committee's work, nearly forty years after it was done, one is struck by the accumulation of detail and the sense of certainty with which the members of the committee pinned down something so ephemeral as the relationship between the quality of family life and the physical setting in which the family lives. There is something absurdly old-fashioned in the effort to quantify this relationship and the stereotype of the Happy Family which it projects. But there is also something quite relevant to the problems of a later day.

Those who drew up the housing standards, like their predecessors, who for the first time in Western social history tried to make changes in the physical conditions of the poor, were reacting to an ethical imperative; namely, that the changes in physical structure were meaningless if they did not enhance and dignify the lives of those affected. The desire to improve one's chances and to open the possibilities of a different style of life, at least for one's children, is shared by the great majority of people who seek to move into better urban housing at the present time.

Major social problems in the cities arise from the weakness of the normative figures of the past: the schoolteacher, the policeman, the cleric, the employer, even the landlord (who imposed budgeting, a requirement of an urban society, on the displaced agricultural workers who thronged to the city). Even while anthropologists proclaim that many alternative modes of family organization are found in stable societies, the people who move into government-supported housing demand that their project encourage "normal" American family life more effectively than the casually downtrodden sections of the city from which they come. Naturally, the aspirants to government-aided housing hope that tenant selectivity will be sufficiently free to allow *them* to enter; but if tenant selection is too free, indiscriminate, the very families who are most likely to benefit from housing will eschew it. Once they have moved in, their standards for conformity and selectivity become more rigid, for they have learned how much damage can be done to the normative possibilities of a decent, new apartment house by even a single destructive family.

The amount of deviation from the idealized "normal" family which is acceptable in any given housing project is a function largely of its location. If the development is in an area with a tradition of bohemianism, families seeking self-enhancement will freely enter a development with a reputation for family deviation that would scare them away in a more conventional area of the city. But there are limits to the amount of deviation which will be acceptable anywhere. Although it may seem pretentious to say so, no greater error can be made with respect to social policy in housing than to allow libertarian principles to impose the cost of one's conscience on those who must live with its consequences.

The question of who shall benefit from government assistance to housing has a second part. Social policy must be concerned not only with those who become initially eligible, but also with the question of who remains eligible and on what terms. As this examination has disclosed, the admission of people to governmental help involves the application of standards that are somewhat ambiguous. Once admitted, however, the resident feels that his status has been established. To deprive him of a benefit bestowed seems a far less equivocal injustice than refusing to admit him in the first place.

Those who concern themselves with the development of social policy, to mitigating the hardships caused by economic pressures, have therefore found the extension of tenure one of their most satisfying activities. The continuance of entitlement to government housing assistance is a special case of the general question of tenure.

To begin with, courts have increasingly found themselves reluctant actually to order evictions from rented homes, even for such summary delinquencies as the failure to pay rent. New York City established a special Housing Court in the Lindsay era, where all cases involving landlords and tenants were handled; it has been reported that the Mayor suggested to those whom he appointed to that bench that it was not in the public interest to put families out on the sidewalk even for nonpayment of rent. Certain of the Hearing Officers have been heard to say that they *never* evict anyone, not even for that offense. In the case of those supported by public assistance, social policy has decreed that eviction for nonpayment of rent should be allowed to happen only in the most unusual cases. If a tenant spends his rent allotment for goods and services other than shelter (in one of the several states which provide for a basic living allowance plus a payment for rent up to an administrative maximum), the welfare authorities will customarily issue a second check to cover the rent and prevent eviction. Sometimes a third check will be issued. In principle, the federal government penalizes those states who try to protect the owner who rents to welfare recipients by issuing checks payable jointly to landlord and tenant; if these exceed 10 percent of the total checks issued, the excess may be deducted from the total of federal grants. In any case, the issuance of so-called two-party checks does not protect the owner against rent delinquency. The forging of the owner's endorsement on the check is commonplace. It involves merely a somewhat higher than usual cashing charge by the grocer or other tradesman who accepts the instrument from the tenant.

Taking its cue, no doubt, from these local practices, and desiring, in all probability, to avoid the appearance of heartlessness, HUD itself issued draft eviction regulations in the late spring of 1976. They stipulated that those enjoying federal housing benefits could not be evicted for nonpayment of rent without a full evidentiary hearing. In most jurisdictions, rent cases are summary proceedings. It is the tenant's responsibility, by producing rent receipts or canceled checks, to prove that he or she actually paid the rent which the landlord alleges not to have been paid. The shift in burden of proof is no trivial matter. An evidentiary proceeding requires witnesses and preparation, and delays in court and requests for adjournments become inevitable.

The immediate impact of this social policy on the economics of housing has been the discouragement of new ownership of and investment in housing. Lest one assume that this effect is felt only by private, profit-motivated builders, it must be stressed that the need to live within the limits of received income afflicts public housing authorities as much as the greediest of profiteers. One indirect result of more tender attitudes toward rent delinquency is a reduction in the real or potential housing supply. Both public and private investors hesitate to commit resources to an increasingly hazardous enterprise.

The ironies do not stop here. One must also consider the effect of a merciful social policy toward rent evasion on those who are its beneficiaries. Stepping back a moment, one might re-examine the reason for the national government's resistance to the issuance of two-party rent checks. The policy, it should be noted, was established in the early days of the federal assumption of a large part of the welfare burden, on the theory that welfare recipients should be treated with dignity in the allocation of welfare payments. This means, in the context of the law, that the recipient is to be treated precisely like the recipient of all other income, and that he or she must learn to budget and control expenditures like the rest of the population. The avoidance of the consequence of failure to budget rent services, however humane its purpose, undermines the very spirit of individual responsibility which welfare policy was intended to foster. Ironically, no real choice exists for welfare officials. If they refuse to make good the delinquent rent, they will in any case not leave the family or its furniture on the sidewalk. At greater expense they would move the unfortunates to a new apartment, provide a new security deposit and a new first month's rental, and simply start the process all over again at a new location. Thus, social policy mitigates economics by impairing some of the goals that it sets for itself.

But if the termination for nonpayment of rent is more difficult than it once was, its difficulties are as nothing compared with the conflict between social policy and housing economics (and between one social policy and another) in the case of more subtle conflicts between the tenure of the tenant and the owner's use of his property.

The most significant loss of tenure from the point of view of productive social policy is the termination of tenancy which results from the inability or unwillingness of a housing resident to conform to a mode of behavior which does not endanger his neighbors. Once again, the subject seems too inhuman to discuss among liberal-minded believers in the natural goodness or at least the limitless perfectibility of this happy species. The facts are, however, that among the occupants of any housing project there are likely to be at least a few households whose children constitute a menace, at least to the old people in the project or to other, possibly smaller children. It would be heartening to report that the staffs of housing projects are graced by the presence of social workers with great dedication and the talent to turn these juvenile nuisances into jovial good neighbors. There are, one supposes, a few such. But the great majority of housing developments lack such talented staff, and after a few bicycles have been stolen, a few younger kids have been beaten and robbed, a few older persons have had their money snatched or their groceries grabbed from them and been knocked down, and a few housing managerial assistants threatened and humiliated with unpleasant language and gestures, and after the watchmen, guards, and housing police have exercised their persuasive or deterrent arts, and the conditions continue, there seems no alternative for the survival of the housing project but to evict the household, some of whose members have proved incorrigible at our present stage of correctional art.

No one relishes the prospect of evicting failed households from housing developments. The process surely does not solve the problem family's problem. But like many another practical public act which falls short of the ideal program of the philosopher king, it does at least remove the threat to others in the development. Incidentally, the same act suggests that part of every large city will have to remain available for *anyone* to live in, however minimal his standards of self-discipline. In short, until society has found a way to make its members live within what might be called a code of tolerable urban behavior, large cities can provide a measure of safety for the majority of their residents only by including a semi-permanent slum within their boundaries. Once again, no one likes to admit that we cannot do better; but matters are only made worse by the unrealistic claim that we can.

In any case, the process of removing difficult and dangerous families from housing developments by the process of eviction for reasons other than nonpayment of rent (happily, many problem families are so obliging as to become rent-delinquent as well as behavior-delinquent) has become a very difficult business. The federal courts have ruled that they can be removed only after a long process which includes an evidentiary hearing, at which those who have been offended must testify. Since the proceedings are far from instantaneous, and both alleged offender and offendee live at the same address, the prospect of testifying is somewhat frightening to the very persons whose safety is in question. The social policy of providing everyone with a measure of protection against unjust accusation has interfered with the social policy of offering every family who can take advantage of it peacefully a decent, safe, and sanitary home in a suitable living environment. There is, obviously, not only no simple answer to this implicit conflict in social values, but probably no final answer at all. That we have not achieved perfection as societal Solomons, however, should not prevent us from redressing a balance which seems to have gone somewhat askew.

Incidentally, the balance between tenure and the development of a housing program is thrown somewhat askew by the change from contract to statutory tenure, particularly in those jurisdictions in which rent control threatens to become a permanent condition. Under most landlord-tenant law, the basic notion is that the relationship is defined by the contract of lease. When the lease terminates at the end of whatever term of years it provides, the tenant must surrender the premises if the owner so desires. This rule is often a harsh one, particularly so when the occupancy of the rented premises is essential to the family livelihood: the tenant-farmer, for example. British statute law, in the early nineteenth century, modified the absolute reliance on contract terms in the case of farm properties, and provided some equitable adjustment, at least, to compensate the tenant-farmer for improvements made by him to the farmlands.

In the case of rented residential property, a tenant at the end of the term of lease may simply refuse to leave the premises. In these cases, the owner must promptly bring a so-called holdover proceeding in many jurisdictions. If the court adjudicates that the tenant has no right to occupy the property, he must leave. While no statistics have been gathered on this question—and gathering them would be an extremely difficult if not an impossible task—it is the impression among many observers of American housing that judges have become increasingly ready to extend the period of continued tenancy *after* the expiration of the lease, in order to mitigate the hardships inflicted by the occasion of the termination of tenure. In some cases, of course, this mitigation of the tenant's hardship shifts the hardship to the owner. Not only may the owner be restrained from collecting a higher rent for his premises; he may be prevented even from using them for his own purposes.

In the case of rent control, the contract tenure is replaced by a statutory tenure. Rent control seeks to retain in the rental market all the units which are subject to it, because the removal of units from the supply increases the pressure on those who demand housing. Presumably, they are already at a disadvantage by the short supply which is usually a legal precondition for the application of rent control by statute. Accordingly, rent control laws inhibit the normal right of an owner to demolish and rebuild housing accommodations.

The rent control law usually stipulates the terms on which tenants can be evicted in order to make demolition or substantial rehabilitation possible. At one time, in many local areas, owners were able to recover possession on a showing of their intention to rebuild or rehabilitate. After the tenants were uprooted, some builders failed to accomplish their intended rebuilding. To correct this abuse, the repossession regulations have become so severe that they lend themselves to artful manipulation by tenants and their attorneys. In effect, these have gone so far beyond the extension of the rights of tenure to create a whole new right to property—the right of occupancy—which, in order to avoid interminable delays, must be bought up by the owner of a fee title in order for him to demolish and construct what may be a substantial addition to the housing supply. It is not unusual for tenants to sell this statutory right of tenure for $30,000, all of which (above his cost of moving) represents gain to the tenant who paid nothing to acquire the right in the first place.

Clearly, then, the social policy consideration which stiffened the terms of tenure, both contract and, particularly, statutory tenure, have had the effect of shaping the economics of housing, by making its ownership less attractive and more heavily burdened.

Finally, social policy comes to the third of its major issues: What shall be the form of the community to be determined by the application of housing-economic intervention?

As indicated in the discussion of the selection of those entitled to benefit from overt government assistance in housing, a generally agreed-upon objective of housing social policy is that it shall not be segregated, at least not by the deliberate exclusionary policy of others. But this statement of general purpose falls far short of a full explanation of the direction of social policy. It does not, for example, indicate whether there will be an effort to promote the neighboring of people of different economic levels, nor does it define the proper level of effort to be put into encouraging the neighboring of people of widely disparate ages. Advocates of social policy support contrasting theories about the typical desires of older people. Some claim that older people like to find themselves integrated with younger families and, particularly, with children. Others maintain that this is what many older people say they want, but that in fact the continuing presence of children wearies and sometimes frightens them.

If, contrarily, it is argued that the purpose of community is to provide alternatives which may be chosen by the affected persons, an implicit statement is being made about the size of the community. Small communities, in which neighboring is fostered by physical propinquity and by small, discrete units of commercial enterprise as contrasted with large, anonymous supermarkets, promote interrelationships between people at the expense of diversity. The promise of major diversities in ethnic and national background, language, race, and cultural interest seems finally reserved for the very largest cosmopolitan environments. But the larger the cosmopolitan community which social policy seeks to preserve for its unique cultural display, the more difficult the task of social policy in overcoming the urban economic problems which lie ahead in the remaining quarter of this century.

Social policy that favors cultural diversity cannot overlook the technological changes that have made the urban concentration of light industry no longer attractive, or the impact on the big-city economies of the formidable competition posed by small-town factories, now that truck highways have provided an elasticity in freight movement that steel-railed transport cannot match. Social policy that seeks to provide low-rent housing in the major cities because they contain a large low-income population must contend with the economic fact that the populations can no longer be put to work in the largest conurbations, which have lost their industrial attractiveness for both old and new enterprises.

Some urge that social policy should prepare the population for entry into a post-industrial era in which employment will be more highly concentrated in service jobs than in the production of goods. Nevertheless, no one has designed a bridge from the *now* to the *then*. Will the post-industrial society find an economic basis for maintaining the urban concentrations of population? If not, nothing can stop the development of new and much smaller urban centers, reproducing the cultural intensity and diversity of the larger cities but somehow miraculously avoiding their offsetting miseries, makes sense. This refers, somewhat obliquely, to the "New Towns" notion, a policy followed with periodic enthusiasm in the United Kingdom. The supporters of the New Towns policy suggest that careful planning will make possible the creation of a sound environment on vacant land in which industry, housing, and commercial and recreational activities will be combined in felicitous measure, on a scale which will avoid the inhumanities of the great cities but foster some of the intercultural, interpersonal choices that to many contemporaries makes urban life preferable to the isolated farm or the small village. The basic assumption in the New Towns movement is that the physical arrangement of space—open and covered—exercises a major impact on the quality of human life, and that the application of wise generosity to the design of space will itself cure societal ills. In fact, the extent to which New Towns have been able to cure societal ills depends more significantly on the fact that the socially incapacitated have usually been left behind in the older cities. The New Towns in Britain, for all their rationalism, have fostered a population mix which closely resembles that of the American suburbs which were brought into existence, New Towns proponents say scornfully, by the irrational admiration of automotive transportation and the profit-motivated proliferation of the high loan-to-value ratio of the FHA-insured mortgage.

It is somewhat uncanny that two forms of settlement—the one designed by rational forces exclusively and the other allegedly by irrational forces exclusively—should in the end resemble each other so much in their population mix and their structural form. Naturally, there will be objectors to this statement, who would argue that some of the U.K. New Towns (Cumbernauld, near Glasgow, is one, or at least its town center is one) do not physically resemble American new suburbs. When one points out that even Cumbernauld has managed to draw from Glasgow precisely the same kinds of people and the same industries that Stamford, Connecticut, has drawn from New York City, one hears that at least the New Towns of the U.K. are free of dependence on the individually owned motorcar. This statement rather reliably dates the speaker's last visit to a British New Town; those that were designed to be impenetrable to the motorcar have had to be remodeled to come to term with it. The attractions of automotive mobility seem universal at this period of human history.

In any case, if the low-skilled worker is not to be useful in the New Towns, social policy raises the alarming question of where indeed he is to be housed with his family, and how, without a serious job opportunity and the example of other authority figures who reinforce the notion of the dignity of work, he is to be peacefully assimilated into the new communities, whether urban, suburban, or Novo Ordine.

The basic question in social policy really cannot be deferred any longer. It is the question of who is to decide what forms of community are the more desirable in general, and where each of these specific forms is to be created. The basic question of social policy is, like most other basic questions, wreathed in ironies. Decisions on the fundamental social policies of a nation may demand abandonment of the political procedures of a free, popularly controlled government. Even so clear-cut an issue as the abolition of slavery involved Americans in a deadly civil war. The definition of the shape of the ideal American community would seem a much more complex issue, lacking any agreed-upon forum or level of government where it might be resolved. Those who advocate a decentralization of governmental authority, and hence would appear to support the resolution by local governments of the shape of their ideal communities, are often the same people who wish the most striking changes in which that form should be cast. They demand local control because they are suspicious of centralized bureaucracy with its technologically trained specialists, and at the same time they must be fearful of that same local control because it is all too likely to be cautious and conservative in its approach to major social problems. Also, clearly, local government lacks the resources necessary to deal with the poverty that generally results from its own economic helplessness. Whereas only a few years ago it was possible to claim that local poverty was the result of maldistribution of resources within the locality, or of some local moral shortcoming which might be called "a lack of commitment," it has now become all too plain that local poverty arises from fundamental economic considerations which are well outside the power of local people to cure. They may even be beyond the power of the national government to cure, even should one assume that the national government—many of whose constituent states compete with each other—is prepared to use its powers for curative purposes.

The federal government, then, is to be asked to provide the economic fodder on which the idealized local community is to be nourished, but the local people will continue to try to hold in their hands the final control over what is to be done because, after all, the congressional legislators who establish the federal law do represent local constituencies. Out of this swirling current of purposes has come revenue sharing. In theory the government, the national government, provides the economic means because its taxes are drawn from the nation as a whole, but it is to permit local government to use these means as the local people see fit.

Only it does not work that way. Nor can it. For the very same reasons that influenced the formulation of housing social policy in the first instance, the national government continues to impose requirements that are essentially moral in nature and determine social policy in ways which impede the achievement of the economic goals. The present balance of responsibility between local and central government is frequently an awkward one. The federal government imposes standards, for example, on prevailing wages which effectively mandate the use of union labor and prevent local governments from initiating training programs with housing grants. Or the federal government imposes income limitations which, established in the rigid pursuit of the piety of helping the very poor first, militate against the very economic mingling which the local government may be seeking to achieve. Or the federal government, relentlessly pursuing the goal of personal mobility without economic limitations, may, in fact, be so discouraging to the prospect of continuing subsidization that local housing efforts may be unable to attract capital. In short, the alignment of the varied social purposes which are an inevitable part of a housing program will require a collaboration between federal and local aims and policies which Americans cannot be said to have achieved. In fact, they are scarcely prepared to discuss the problem except in terms of righteousness which they delight in espousing orally but shrink from in practice.

5

MEETING
THE CHALLENGE

From time to time, most recently in 1965, the national government has sought to quantify the nation's housing need. The 1965 figures were used to guide the government in intensifying the allocation of resources to improve the material standards of lagging groups in the population, a goal then described as the Great Society. The figures were not particularly convincing. Like all such quantifications, they were based on projections of family formation in the next fifteen years and on a theory of the rate of obsolescence of existing and occupied standard-quality housing. Most uncertain of all, the estimates were based on notions, half expressed, of where in the United States housing would be needed to accommodate population shifts. The precision of the estimates of housing need was, then, largely exaggerated. Only in a much more rigid society than that of the United States could anyone predict with accuracy the housing need fifteen years in the future or judge fairly where the housing should go. Even in the Soviet Union, where government policy more effectively regulates the lives of the citizenry, and where the priorities of housing policy have been relatively clear—e.g., to assist in the development of industrial capacity beyond the Urals—people have a way of thwarting government intentions. Despite all government sanctions against such a movement, good Soviet citizens manage to augment the population of Leningrad, simply because talented people want to move there, and the managers of the state industries in Leningrad are delighted to welcome them with appropriate paperwork.

Given all of these limitations on forecasting, and the further complexities set forth earlier in the discussion of the purposes of housing, it is nevertheless possible to proclaim a rough estimate of the minimum and maximum limits of housing production in the United States. Unless there are drastic changes in what are now the current levels of demand and supply because of unexpected variations in some of the assumptions discussed above, continuing failure to produce at least 1.5 million units of housing in the United States per year—whether by new construction or substantial rehabilitation—will leave a growing number of Americans living at a standard increasingly far below that established by local laws. On the other extreme, a production stimulus which would result in the development of more than 3 million units a year (units as complicated and expensive as those currently being produced), together with the associated packages of utility and social amenity, would strain the production and credit facilities of the country, were this rate of production to be maintained for more than a year or two. And much of this construction would be misplaced.

It can also be predicted, within a rough margin of error, that the low-side target of 1.5 million per year will not be met unless a significant amount of subsidization in the marketplace is provided for those families whose financial ability to use standard housing is limited by low income. This formulation avoids any mention of the social value of giving low-income people an opportunity to live in decent housing in suitable neighborhoods, but the omission does not mean that those who adopt the national policy should be similarly narrow in their perspectives. In addition to the market subsidies, which can in theory be provided, whether to the consumers or to the producers, additional market encouragement must be provided, or the housing will not be built. The discussion in these pages makes possible an outline form of what an effective national housing program should be in order to keep the production above 1.5 million units per year, and yet below the 3 million level which might be induced by unwise policies. Incidentally, policies to increase the housing supply so dramatically are not necessarily spawned by benevolence. They may be intended to bring a glow of induced health to a naturally lagging economy.

The discussion is not intended to produce the language of a housing bill. Nor does it recommend drastic changes in current legislation where these are not necessary. The present Housing and Community Development Act contains many of the essential requirements of such an instrument. The discussion does attempt, however, to provide a structure of ideas in which the essential elements of a housing bill are set forth; it should, at a minimum, explain why these elements are essential and provide something of a consistent picture of what makes for housing production and what impedes it; what makes for the availability of such housing to persons of limited income and what impedes that.

The first element in a national housing program is the emergence of sound patterns of ownership. Legislation must provide suitable motivations with which to support and encourage that ownership. The first notable gap in present federal housing legislation is its failure to support public governmental ownership of rental housing. This defect must be remedied. Low-income families will continue to need rental housing in many parts of the nation, and public ownership offers one mode of ownership by which this commodity can be supplied directly. The public authority provides some guarantee of continuing ownership. Yet the present housing act makes no provision for the allocation of Section 8 rental subsidies to new publicly owned housing units. The combination of an allocation of Section 8 units with the tax-exemption feature on the interest paid by local housing authorities on their borrowings would enable public housing authorities to raise funds in the capital market.

The legalization of subsidy allocations to public authorities does not mean that public ownership should be the only mode of ownership encouraged by the federal legislation. Nor does it mean that the organization of the public authorities must be limited to its present form.

The vast majority of the governmental housing authorities today are municipal authorities (there are a few county authorities). It would probably be of some help in finding appropriate sites for low-income housing developments if the states themselves were permitted to institute housing authorities and empowered to build and operate developments with federal subsidies. The state authorities would have greater power than city authorities to build outside local municipal limits. Regional housing authorities, empowered to build anywhere within the regional limits, could come into existence only following the execution of interstate compacts, but these might be encouraged by providing special additional federal subsidies to replace local taxation in the case of developments owned by regional authorities. The obvious advantage of the regional authority would be its power to build for low-income families wherever in a region such housing would seem suitable, not only for local residents but also for low income families now residing elsewhere. Since the board of a regional authority would probably be appointed by the governors of the states involved, it would in the end not be totally free to offend local people with impunity, but its goals and perspectives would be different from those of purely local officials. Naturally, this proposal will meet with opposition, but it provides a practical instrument (surely not the only one) for carrying forward doctrines with respect to the placement of low-income housing which are now generally articulated by the federal courts and embodied by federal regulation. The nation lacks any feasible method of implementation under present law.

In the larger cities, too, there is room for innovation in the nature of the local authority. Taking our model from the British, there seems to be no reason why a city with a population of one million or more should have only one housing authority. Local boroughs or wards might be empowered to construct or operate housing developments, perhaps using technical services provided by the city or state authority, services which would be paid for from the mortgage proceeds. The municipal or state authority might also be responsible for funding the local project, an operation which would presumably be relatively easy because its funds would be secured by the same pledge of federal Section 8 revenues which would put the larger authorities into the money market.

The local character of management which such an innovation would provide might allay some of the resentment of the public ownership instrument occasioned by an authority which is somewhat remote from the local scene. Contrarily, the threat that the municipal or regional authority would construct low-income housing if the borough or ward authority failed to act might well persuade reluctant local authorities to move forward.

It is a matter of utmost importance for housing in the major cities that something be done for rural housing, with emphasis on housing for agricultural workers. The nation now permits the introduction of significant numbers of foreign agricultural workers to harvest crops in Florida and the western states near Mexico. At the same time it encourages the clustering of unemployed citizens with roughly similar background and ability in the cities, where they eke out a miserable existence on welfare payments. Rural reconstruction to make life attractive in the countryside would encourage the return of these urban residents to a type of work they know better. The requirements of such reconstruction are vast; housing is by no means the only important part of such a program, but it is an essential part, as are schools, shopping, and recreational facilities. None should underestimate the local resistance to any program to make the countryside attractive to the underemployed urban populations that might become farm workers: the fear of rural governments that they might be required to provide schools, hospitals, and other structures staffed with locally paid workers constitutes a monumental block. Nevertheless, the federal government can take a major part in this effort through direct housing production and ownership—temporary, perhaps—with the possibility of ultimate sale to the residents remaining the goal of rural housing. This does not mean the construction of high-rise housing projects in the agricultural regions. It does mean the construction of well-designed, simple, carefully planned one-family or perhaps two-family structures, combining with the housing program pattern of fiscal assistance to local governments. Though on its surface a rural program, nothing else would be quite so helpful to the older cities, whose primary economic problem today is the continued presence of families who can find no economically productive work where they are located.

The public housing program that evolved in the 1937 National Housing Act made possible local borrowing for publicly owned housing construction by pledging federal contributions which were large enough to service the debt. This formula would still work to raise capital funds, but the operating costs of public housing have soared, requiring the supplementing of the basic capital subsidy with new and somewhat haphazard operating subsidies for housing developments long ago completed. The basic housing subsidy now provided in Section 8 of Title II of the National Housing Act is, as we have seen, a subsidy better designed than the annual contributions of public housing to cover rises in operating costs. Public authorities should be allowed to qualify in existing public housing for the same Section 8 subsidies that new privately owned dwellings funded by state borrowing agencies are allowed to qualify for. This would protect local authorities from the effects of cost increases which might otherwise bankrupt them, but it constitutes only a first step toward the control of operating costs. These are a major problem in public housing, even more serious perhaps than is the case with private housing.

To minimize such increases in operating costs new designs of the physical structure are required. Changes are needed in the allocation of costs also, and the pattern of management, including the participation of tenants.

First, public assistance payments must be sufficient to pay a reasonable ratio of the rental cost of subsidized publicly owned housing. Present federal legislation establishes a limit on the percentage of their public assistance grants which welfare families may be charged as rent in public housing. In those states which establish a basic family allowance to which rent cost is added, this offers a windfall. It also means that the public housing authority must rent to such welfare families at an uneconomic rent. These provisions must be changed.

Second, the pernicious practice of including utility costs in rent must be discontinued. Under the present method of including utility charges in the rent, no one has a motive for reducing his consumption or waste of electric power, gas, or heat. The result is markedly higher per capita usage of these services in structures with rent-inclusion than in those where each resident is billed separately. It is, of course, cheaper in the first instance to build with only one electric or gas meter to cover the entire project. At a time when the costs of utility service production remained very stable, the saving in construction costs was significant. That is no longer the case; hydrocarbons, the essential ingredient in the generation of electricity, have tripled in price in the last five years in many parts of the United States. The monthly costs of electric power and gas now dwarf the initial saving. The suggestion that individual households be billed for their utility costs in publicly subsidized or owned housing may raise a specter of cold people and dark houses for those who lack sufficient funds. Actually, public assistance payments that are based on a family budget would include a reasonable provision for utility charges in the development of the budget. Undue waste of these services would exceed the allowances and require the careless family to save the money elsewhere.

Improved design of low-income housing developments involves infinitely more than the installation of separate utility meters. The buildings must be arranged to encourage the assumption of custodial duties by their tenants. Long public hallways which no one cleans except paid staff should be eliminated; entrances to housing developments should be so situated as to minimize the number of paid guards required to patrol them. The open-space design must minimize small fenced-off areas that gather waste paper and prevent easy access for cleaning them. Windowless fire stairs that offer sanctuary for youth gangs and worse can be eliminated by the use of low-rise design. Projects might well be designed to encourage a sense of small-scale neighboring and, perhaps, to subdivide into separate cooperative groupings if the time for such changes becomes propitious.

The national government has done comparatively little to encourage the design and management of public housing. It should support private institutions (and perhaps a national institute) which conduct research in these fields. Brave words have been inserted into housing bills, but the high probability that the research will be fruitless or even frivolous has discouraged actual commitment of funds. Those in charge must be willing to admit that housing will remain excruciatingly expensive so long as present housing code standards remain as high as they are, and that expenditures for research on such intangibles as community design and management will also be high. One worthwhile suggestion, however, may produce substantial economies in compensation.

Finally, the involvement of local private citizens in low-income design and management is important. The objectives are two. Such involvement may help to produce a receptive attitude toward housing in the locality. Of probably even greater importance is the involvement of residents in certain aspects of project management. This involvement will never dissipate the them-us opposition between tenants and authorities which, as we have indicated, is basic to the very relationship between men and property. Tenant participation in management does, however, bring peer-group pressure to bear on the establishment of behavior norms for housing development residents. Increased tenant participation in management will also help in dealing with multiproblem families. Such participation may persuade the courts that actions to eliminate destructive families from housing developments are not necessarily bureaucratic, imperious, or despotic, but may be a matter of community survival.

Tenant participation in management also provides a useful framework for pre-occupancy and post-occupancy training of housing residents. While one may continue to hope that housing will become simpler, requiring less knowledge of complex systems (such as elevators) on the part of those who live in it, training will continue to be necessary simply because many of those moving into new or newly renovated housing have never before been in a similarly complex environment.

In a society that is traditionally committed to the expression of human equality, the design of low-income housing cannot be markedly different from the housing enjoyed by the rest of the population. This suggests that the subsidization of extravagance by property tax and interest deductibility without limit from income taxes probably requires some change. Relatively unimportant differences between low-rent public housing and standard private housing (the lack of closet doors, in early designs, for example) tended to discourage many desirable families from entering public housing. Many of these differences have been eliminated. For those who cannot bring themselves to believe that human nature is essentially angelic, public housing design and location must be good enough so that the fear of losing one's place in it will be an encouragement to some families, at least, to discipline themselves sufficiently to meet the reasonable standards of their neighbors.

General ground rules for public housing must include reliance on a broadened Section 8 subsidy helping *every* family that pays more than 25 percent of its ordinary income to live in a structure whose rent does not exceed "fair market levels." But we have not yet touched on the greatest difficulty in public ownership, or indeed all federally assisted ownership of housing for low- or moderate income families. That question is: where shall the housing be put? To demand a "National Land Use Policy" without suggesting its content is futile. The selection of sites for housing for low-income families has become highly politicized. In a land market in which economic value is largely determined by social considerations, and in which many believe that an acre next to the Rockefellers' estate in Pocantico Hills is *per se* worth more than an acre next to a glue factory or a crematorium, the implications of low-income siting are quite emotional. Those who believe that David Rockefeller should be no more desirable to his prospective neighbors than an unemployed ditch digger with a louder voice and a different vocabulary, will deliberately seek to put low-income public housing where it is not wanted by its neighbors. Smiting the bourgeoisie still appears to the young (and some not quite so young) as a valid expression of egalitarian fervor. Other observers may be less convinced, finding in its indulgence an obstinate strain of oedipal reminiscences.

In any case, on the local scene, the public housing sites (and other sites for low-income families which might be in private hands, though subsidized publicly) should be chosen not for revenge, but with respect to the social and utility packages which low-income families need. Access to jobs should be of primary importance; the proximity of decent schools is equally important.

On the difficult subject of desegregation, both sides—the desegregationists and the integrationists—might be willing to agree that the right to choose between two types of neighborhood might be construed as a natural right of those benefited by housing subsidies. Some housing should be built in areas of minority-group concentration because some minority-group members like to live there. Some housing for low-income minority families might be made available elsewhere, where integration is more likely, because some minority families wish to live *there*. Does any family really want to be told that it cannot live where it wants to (because its presence will tip the balance) or that it must live where it does not want to (because its presence will restore a balance)?

So much for micro-siting. An even more significant factor is what might be called "macro-siting." The absence of any market factor in the decision as to how to apportion federal subsidies between several parts of the nation is underscored by the historic limitation that no single state may obtain more than 15 percent of the public housing annual contributions. Indeed, the relationship between the market demand and the allocation of housing subsidies for the poor is worse than nonexistent. The relationship is perverse, because it is precisely those areas which have the highest concentration of poor people which have the greatest demand for low-rent housing. While it certainly appears sound and humane to build permanent housing where low-income people live, and where the local political climate is far more likely to be receptive to the low-income housing, the construction in such a site may be precisely the *least* humane act in the long-term interest of poor people. In an abstract sense, devoid of political connotations, it might in fact be most desirable not to build low-income housing which would have the effect of anchoring poor people in the very areas of the nation where they have the smallest opportunity for jobs and economic advancement.

The issue posed by this quandary—that the areas most receptive to housing for the poor are precisely the areas from which the poor should be encouraged to move—is like a baseball that is too hot to handle and which thus passes untouched between the representatives of local and national government. It may be of some consolation to recall that this issue of moving populations to areas of greater economic promise is as difficult in other countries as in the United

States. Surely, however, the granting of housing subsidies might be shaped by national statistics on regional unemployment ratios and forecasts of future population growth. Something of this kind of market analysis would surely be required if the low-income housing involved anyone's private investment; the investment would be withheld in the absence of market conditions that promise increased income. Government forecasting has not attained a higher degree of reliability in economics than in weather, but it is hard to resist saying that some forecasting is surely preferable to the current system, which inverts the long-term necessities of population movement and offers continuing poverty in better housing as a substitute for the possibility of higher earnings.

These remarks about the resurrection of public ownership do not mean that private ownership of housing for low-income families should be entirely abandoned. On the contrary, federal housing policy should encourage the development of other, complementary modes of ownership even though the augury based on past experience is generally unfavorable.

The continued use of a flexible consumer subsidy like the present Section 8 subsidy should make it possible for an ownership entity to accommodate low-income families provided only that the owner is able to rent its units within the levels described by the federal government as "fair market levels" for the *locality* in which the housing lies. The meaning of *locality* is clear enough in the case of small settlements which can be regarded as a single market area; its meaning in larger cities could be that the government is willing to pay *anywhere* in the city rents which are fair for the city as a whole. The same words might also be interpreted to mean that the government will pay only those rents which are "fair" within the *specific subsection* in which the beneficiary lives and wants to use his subsidy. Both interpretations are troublesome. In the first case, one might imagine that the subsidy would support grossly excessive rents in depressed areas of the city, with minimal benefit to the quality of the apartments. In the second case, the subsidy would provide no infusion of new money to patch up and hold together aging neighborhoods in which people may want to live. One can hope only that the words of the statute will be interpreted in a way that cuts between the two polar positions, so that the very generous subsidy provided under Section 8 may be made more useful in stabilizing neighborhoods that are suffering from such a dearth of effective demand that their actual rents are essentially unfair.

We have noted that the Section 8 formula provides that the government will reserve the entire rent of a unit to be used by an eligible recipient, even though the recipient himself will be paying at least a part and sometimes nearly all of the rent. The reserve of allocated funds allows the government to respond to increases in operating costs. Its difficulties, in present form, are two. First, the Department of Housing and Urban Development will not permit subsidies to be directed deliberately toward neighborhoods or toward individual pre-existing projects where the financial help is badly needed. The recipient of the housing subsidies is intended to have freedom of choice. The subsidy formula is cast in such a way that it fails to encourage mortgage investment. If the nation wants to stimulate others besides governmental authorities to offer rental accommodations to the poor, it must cast its subsidies in a form that will attract mortgage money. This means, as we have seen, that the subsidies must be set aside by contract for a period long enough to permit full repayment of the mortgage. The present act, to repeat, permits this only for subsidies payable to "State Agencies," not including public housing authorities.

Earlier, it was noted that quasi-public nonprofit ownership has been largely unsuccessful in attracting the same kind of eleemosynary interest in housing that it attracted in the case of health care. Nevertheless, there seems to be ample reason for using federal money to stimulate the formation of nonprofit housing ownership agencies which would, in effect, offer their staffs the same incentives for continued service that government does, and which would yet be free of some of the inflexibilities for which governments are notorious (perhaps not always justly so). Such agencies would offer real risks to the federal government—many would surely go by the board—because they would require advance public funding to take the place of the capital investment that is stimulated by the hope of profit. This advance funding would come only from the government, in much the way, for example, that the funding of Phipps Houses, one of the more successful of such organizations, was received from the estate of Henry Phipps, an associate of Carnegie. One cannot codify the rules under which such nonprofit agencies might be selected for advance funding, but if government ownership is not to be the only developer of housing for low-income families, and if neither tax incentives, as at present, nor large tax-shielded investment profits are possible politically for private profit-motivated owners, then there seems to be no choice other than to take the risks outlined.

A still more important type of ownership emerges from the discussion, however. This is the ownership of simplified housing, urban housing which does not require the payment of third parties for the largest part of the routine maintenance chores. This type of ownership—resident ownership of a two-, three-, or four-family dwelling—has generally been overlooked in the formulation of federal housing policy, just as the factory-built mobile home has been overlooked. The emergence of both of these types of housing without substantial federal assistance indicates the presence of important market forces moving in their direction. One might even go a step further and point out that important cultural forces in the direction of simplification and a reduction of long-accepted standards lie behind both of them. Certainly the forces tending to simplify the industrial process and to lower standards can be attacked from significant cultural vantage points. But both tendencies are, in fact, here. And both represent genuine popular revulsion against aspects of industrial life which were generally assumed to be praiseworthy.

Thus, the emerging success of the very small-scale housing development—sufficiently small to permit the owner to carry out a large part of the maintenance himself and to be a personal beneficiary of the service he provides the other residents—represents a reversion from the large-scale development, highly mechanized, highly unionized, the product of high technology in such matters as the design of reinforced concrete. In other words, the small housing development represents a flight from modernity. Yet it is not so dizzying a flight that it need cause fright to those who praise industrialization. In fact, it can benefit from many of the fruits of industrialization such as the design of concrete planking, but it is industrialization which encourages a small-scale ownership that brings with it a strong infusion of personal contact and personal responsibility.

A serious national effort to encourage this type of housing would involve federal encouragement of local zoning changes to make two-, three-, and four-family homes legal in many local areas where they are currently proscribed in favor of single-family homes. The effort would also encourage changes in building laws so that unrealistic standards can be eliminated; in many jurisdictions, a four-family structure must comply with the same building-code fire-exit provisions as a 400-family structure. Architects must be encouraged to involve themselves in the design and engineering of these small structures which have so far been considered to be beneath their dignity. Mortgage insurance must be made available that would encourage ownership of such structures with largely reduced down payments (provided the owner was required to live in the building). Most particularly, the small multifamily, owner-occupied residence would encourage the emergence of nonwhite housing entrepreneurs. Some might also see in a program to encourage this housing a general deterrent to the spread of rent control, for the inescapably obvious reason that the ratio of renters to owners drops drastically when the standard multifamily residence building drops from an average of fifty rental units per building owner to three units per building owner. Among the renters may, in fact, be members of the owning family.

Finally, with respect to the profit-motivated apartment house owner, there will remain significant sections of the urban and suburban population who will continue to provide a market for his product. The aged, young couples, married and unmarried, the never married, the childless (permanently or newly so)—many of the households which fall into these categories have no desire to own their own homes. Even though they may have the economic means to do so, they choose to invest their capital otherwise. Many of these people want to live in central city locations where the three- or four-family home is ruled out by high land costs. The Section 8 subsidy program will continue (on a larger scale, perhaps) to reduce rents to levels that the low-income people in these market groups can pay. But the subsidies are useless unless there are new apartments—or decently maintained older apartments—to which to apply subsidies. If there is no rental ownership, there is little point in a Section 8 program.

Although rental apartment ownership continues to be needed, current trends indicate that the encouragements to rental ownership are fewer than the discouragements. The consumer movement has made the owners of rental residential property extremely vulnerable to controls. Banks and the life insurance executives who have traditionally provided the capital for their operations are well aware of the threat of rent control. They have been frightened from the apartment house mortgage market by sharp rises in interest rates that have made their long-term non-industrial commitments unwise. Short-term mortgages simply transfer the risk of interest rate changes to the owners and residents of the buildings, who are equally if not more vulnerable. The bankers as well as the life insurance executives have been further dismayed by the dis-intermediation of their depositors who choose to take advantage of higher interest rates elsewhere. In the case of life insurance policy owners, the disintermediation is manifested by a rise in policy loans during periods of high interest. Furthermore, the continued deficits of federal budgets and the ambitious capital investment plans (until very recently) of state and local governments have offered riskless (until very recently) and low-overhead alternatives to apartment house loans. The trend toward expanded consumer loan business by savings depositories is unmistakable. Finally, the socialization of retirement—previously an individual responsibility, largely met by periodic deposits in savings and loan associations and mutual savings banks where the money was available for first-mortgage loans—has directed much of the savings flow into three other channels: government obligations, certain highly regarded common stocks, and, less tastefully, into speculative investments which have attracted the favorable notice of pension fund trustees.

Many commentators have discussed the implications of the growth in pension funds from the points of view of safety for the prospective beneficiaries, of corporate control, of the nature of trustee responsibility, of capital formation for industry. There has been relatively little discussion of the impact of the changes on the savings industry in its relationship to housing. Yet even these few words indicate that rental housing is impossible without entrepreneurs; and there can be no housing entrepreneurs, whether public, private, nonprofit, or in any combination of the three, without a flow of capital resources into housing through the institution of the mortgage. All of these money market trends must be reversed by government action if housing in private hands—particularly rental housing—is to be built.

In this respect two points might be made. One, as Congress has noted in the National Housing and Community Development Act of 1974, is that the government cannot take *all* the risk, as it has for all practical purposes in mortgage insurance. The act provides for a co-insurance program, in which lending institutions must take part of the risk of loss, while the national government absorbs the lion's share (not the cowardly lion's either). Although the issue has been less discussed than it should have been, co-insurance seems a sensible corrective to the excessive, speculative, and frequently disastrous overbuilding that has afflicted the FHA at times like those when President Nixon wanted to put a little pep into the economy. But co-insurance probably results in lower loan-to-value ratios, meaning that mortgages will cover less of the total development cost than in the past. To meet the full cost of development, the owner will have to put up more of his own money as equity (except for the two-, three-, and four-family home owner, who has been apparently excluded from these tasty benefits in the past). But no developer will invest more equity capital in rental housing than he has been accustomed to invest in the past unless he glimpses the possibilities, if not the certainty, of higher tax-sheltered profits. This means, at the very least, that the fair market rents which the national government is prepared to subsidize with a consumer subsidy like Section 8 must provide a level of return that is likely to attract private entrepreneurs. If these rent levels are politically unacceptable (and the present income tax shelter scheme becomes obsolete) the nation will not have private rental housing, but must make do with its government, eleemosynary, or mutually owned alternatives.

Implicit in many of these rough guidelines for a national housing policy is the inexorable connection between the actual cost of the housing development and the practicability of housing policy. American housing costs too much. Much of it is too elaborate in comparison with housing patterns abroad. Simultaneously, the same units may be too skimpy in comparison with luxury housing here. Housing in rental apartments costs more than people are willing to spend, a political fact which results in rent control laws in which the price of the housing unit tends to be unrelated in practice to the costs incurred in keeping it on the market (even though rent control may provide theoretical hardship relief). It costs too much, particularly, when one includes in the calculation the tremendous investments required to provide the utility and social packages which are needed with the housing. The balance has not yet been struck between reinvestment to modernize existing cities and new investment in newer cities where the utility package costs will be tremendous but where there is at least a promise of greater economic activity and a more liberating social future. Perhaps the balance cannot be struck with the tools now at hand, or within the framework of a government responsive to free elections in which certain unspeakables concerning the movement of population must remain forever unuttered.

The ultimate American housing challenge is whether to wait for better answers or continue as best we can with what we have. It is unlikely that the next few years will see the renascence of public housing as it should be, or the development of a better capital market for housing investment, or a sounder strategy for allocating resources today for the demographic pattern of twenty years in the future. Despite these shortcomings, despite the persistence of significant inequalities, and performance that is in many ways extremely wasteful, government activity in American housing must continue if the low-income family is to make progress toward attaining a decent home. It is regrettable that the nation has not been able to find a swifter and less wasteful, expensive, and haphazard process for achieving this end. It is particularly regrettable that no guarantee can be found that the family assisted with so much effort and at such high public cost is in fact living in the place where its future will be most hopeful and through the exercise of its own informed choice. But then it cannot be proved, in any case, that a decent home will be of real significance to any specific family which does not already have one. We operate under a social imperative which makes the nation feel—not equally perhaps, and not always, but on the whole at least—that a major effort to improve the status of those with poor housing is worthwhile. And in somewhat the same frame of mind, we must assume that if it is good that all people should have at least one offering of a decent home, it is probably good that we should not wait to offer that opportunity until all problems have been solved, all injustices eliminated, all false steps prevented, all waste abolished. This falls far short of a utopian solution to the nation's housing challenge, but it can safely be said that the defects of America's housing program are not ascribable simply to a lack of national will to correct them. The answers, if there are answers, are difficult, complex, and elusive; and the few models abroad to which the American observer might look in the expectation of more nearly perfect solutions generally turn out, on closer inspection, to be not quite as described, or irrelevant to the American situation, or just as unsatisfactory to a large part of their reputedly satisfied population as America's housing remains to a part of its people.